# SPRITZ!

**SPRITZ**

Copyright © 2025 by Cider Mill Press Book Publishers LLC.

This is an officially licensed book by Cider Mill Press Book Publishers LLC.

All rights reserved under the Pan-American and International Copyright Conventions.

No part of this book may be reproduced in whole or in part, scanned, photocopied, recorded, distributed in any printed or electronic form, or reproduced in any manner whatsoever, or by any information storage and retrieval system now known or hereafter invented, without express written permission of the publisher, except in the case of brief quotations in critical articles and reviews.

The scanning, uploading, and distribution of this book via the internet or via any other means without permission of the publisher is illegal and punishable by law. Please support authors' rights, and do not participate in or encourage piracy of copyrighted materials.

13-Digit ISBN: 978-1-40035-115-2
10-Digit ISBN: 1-40035-115-4

This book may be ordered by mail from the publisher. Please include $5.99 for postage and handling. Please support your local bookseller first!

Books published by Cider Mill Press Book Publishers are available at special discounts for bulk purchases in the United States by corporations, institutions, and other organizations. For more information, please contact the publisher.

Cider Mill Press Book Publishers
"Where good books are ready for press"
501 Nelson Place
Nashville, Tennessee 37214

cidermillpress.com

Typography: Adobe Garamond Pro, Aire Bold Pro, Poppins

Image Credits: Pages 7, 43, 107, 108, and 132 used under official license from Shutterstock. Page 11 courtesy of Unsplash. All other photos courtesy of Cider Mill Press.

Printed in Malaysia

24 25 26 27 28 PJM 5 4 3 2 1
First Edition

# SPRITZ!

**CHEERS TO 100+ REFRESHING, SPARKLING COCKTAILS**

# CONTENTS

| | |
|---|---|
| INTRODUCTION | 6 |
| EXCITE | 8 |
| REFRESH | 64 |
| RELAX | 104 |
| ELEVATE | 150 |
| CELEBRATE | 186 |
| INDEX | 215 |

# INTRODUCTION

There is no group of cocktails that can match everything the spritz is capable of. Charged with bubbles and centered around palate-awakening ingredients, a spritz provides excitement, building anticipation for what's next. Light and low-ABV, a spritz guarantees refreshment and relaxation. Always appearing in eye-catching hues and sleek glassware, a spritz adds an air of elegance and a festive spirit wherever it appears.

Because of these enviable attributes, the mixology world has started to pay considerable attention to the spritz, pushing the envelope in terms of what it can be.

Originally, a spritz was a straightforward mixture of wine and soda water. When liqueurs, particularly a bitter red Italian aperitif such as Campari or Aperol, entered the picture, the spritz began its march to the top of everyone's wishlist for a host of occasions.

As it is such a good fit in so many instances, more imaginative bartenders began wondering what else it might be capable of enhancing. Some mixologists have started employing stronger spirits such as gin and mezcal in their spritzes, creating drinks that have a bit more backbone, and can no longer be brushed aside by aficionados as unserious fare. Others have turned to infusions to amp up the aesthetics and further whet the appetite. In both instances, these innovations retain the light, refreshing, and effervescent characteristics that are fundamental to the concept of the spritz, but have taken the category far from the wine-and-soda space it originally inhabited.

This book collects the very best of these novel creations, as well as the classics that drew everyone's interest initially. From simple, straightforward serves to impressive concoctions that feature advanced techniques such as fat washing and sous vide, there's a cocktail within for every preference and occasion, all united by one of the drinks world's most powerful truths: bubbles make everything better.

# EXCITE

WHEN THE LABORS OF THE DAY ARE PAST AND AN EVENING FILLED WITH FAMILY, FRIENDS, AND GREAT FOOD IS AHEAD, IT'S THE PERFECT TIME TO TURN TO THE SPRITZ, AS IT IS CHARGED WITH CELEBRATORY EFFERVESCENCE AND COMPOSED OF INGREDIENTS KNOWN FOR THEIR PALATE-AWAKENING PROPERTIES.

# Aperol Spritz

*The official drink of summer has soared in popularity over the past decade and for good reason—it's perfect.*

**GLASSWARE:** WINEGLASS

**GARNISH:** ORANGE SLICES

**3 OZ. PROSECCO**

**2 OZ. APEROL**

**1 OZ. SELTZER**

Fill the wineglass with ice and add the ingredients in the order they are listed.

Gently lift the Aperol with a bar spoon, garnish with the orange slice, and enjoy.

# Go Ahead, Romeo

*There's something especially exciting about a drink whose character changes over time, and the Go Ahead, Romeo is just such a concoction. Made with prosecco and Aperol Ice Cubes, the sweet, citrusy notes of the Aperol will make themselves increasingly known as the ice begins to melt, changing both the color and flavor of this delicious drink.*

**GLASSWARE:** BRANDY SNIFTER

**GARNISH:** ORANGE TWIST

| | |
|---|---|
| 6 | **APEROL ICE CUBES (SEE RECIPE)** |
| 4 | **OZ. PROSECCO** |

Place the Aperol Ice Cubes in the snifter and pour the prosecco over them.

Garnish with the orange twist and enjoy.

**APEROL ICE CUBES:** Combine ¼ cup Aperol and ¾ cup water, pour the mixture into ice cube trays, and freeze until solid.

# Elderflower Spritz

*The rosemary and grapefruit peel key this simple drink, releasing a bittersweet, herbal aroma that draws one into every sip.*

**GLASSWARE:** WINEGLASS

**GARNISH:** NONE

| | |
|---|---|
| 1 | SPRIG OF FRESH ROSEMARY |
| 1 | STRIP OF GRAPEFRUIT PEEL |
| 1½ | OZ. ELDERFLOWER LIQUEUR, CHILLED |
| | PROSECCO, CHILLED, TO TOP |

Chill the wineglass in the freezer.

Rub the rosemary and strip of grapefruit peel around the inside of the wineglass and set them aside.

Pour the liqueur into the glass and top with prosecco.

Gently add ice to the cocktail, place the rosemary and strip of grapefruit peel on top, and enjoy.

**DEMERARA SYRUP:** Place 1 cup water in a saucepan and bring it to a boil. Add ½ cup Demerara sugar and 1½ cups sugar and stir until they have dissolved. Remove the pan from heat and let the syrup cool completely before using or storing.

# Ananda Spritz

*When you see spritz, you expect something that is light, simple, and refreshing. The Ananda Spritz is all of those things, but it takes a fascinating route to that destination, brilliantly incorporating darker-hued elements such as bourbon and amaro.*

**GLASSWARE:** COUPE

**GARNISH:** EDIBLE FLOWER BLOSSOMS

| | |
|---|---|
| 5 | **PINEAPPLE CHUNKS** |
| 1½ | **OZ. KNOB CREEK BOURBON** |
| 1 | **OZ. AMARO NONINO** |
| 3 | **DASHES OF ANGOSTURA BITTERS** |
| ½ | **OZ. DEMERARA SYRUP (SEE RECIPE)** |
| ½ | **OZ. FRESH LEMON JUICE** |
| ½ | **OZ. PINEAPPLE JUICE** |
| ¾ | **OZ. SPARKLING WINE** |

Place the pineapple in a cocktail shaker and muddle it.

Add all of the remaining ingredients, except for the sparkling wine, fill the shaker two-thirds of the way with ice, and shake until chilled.

Strain the cocktail into the coupe and top with the sparkling wine.

Garnish with edible flower blossoms and enjoy.

# Apple of Your Eye

*The light touch of the Apple Syrup ties all of the flavors together, and the double dose of bitters is sure to invigorate your palate.*

**GLASSWARE:** FOOTED PILSNER GLASS

**GARNISH:** LEMON WHEEL, LIME WHEEL, APPLE SLICES, FRESH MINT

| | |
|---|---|
| 2 | CUCUMBER RIBBONS |
| 2 | OZ. PIMM'S NO. 1 |
| ¾ | OZ. HENDRICK'S GIN |
| | DASH OF ANGOSTURA BITTERS |
| 2 | DASHES OF PEYCHAUD'S BITTERS |
| ½ | OZ. FRESH LEMON JUICE |
| ½ | OZ. FRESH LIME JUICE |
| 1 | OZ. APPLE SYRUP (SEE RECIPE) |
| | GINGER BEER, TO TOP |

Place the cucumber ribbons in the footed pilsner glass.

Place all of the remaining ingredients, except for the ginger beer, in a cocktail shaker, fill it two-thirds of the way with ice, and shake vigorously 20 times.

Strain into the glass and top with ginger beer.

Garnish with the lemon wheel, lime wheel, apple slices, and fresh mint and enjoy.

**APPLE SYRUP:** Slice an apple and place it in a medium saucepan with 1 cup water, 1 cup sugar, and ½ teaspoon pure vanilla extract. Bring to a boil over medium heat, reduce the heat to medium-low, and simmer for 5 minutes. Remove the pan from heat and let the syrup cool completely. Strain before using or storing.

# Botanical Garden Spritz

*A swarm of floral and herbal notes makes this one as pleasant as a greenhouse in the middle of winter, a sign of life in an otherwise desolate space.*

**GLASSWARE:** WINEGLASS

**GARNISH:** FRESH DILL, CUCUMBER RIBBON, EDIBLE FLOWER BLOSSOMS

- ¾ OZ. LONDON DRY GIN
- ¾ OZ. DRY VERMOUTH
- ¾ OZ. KAMM & SONS BRITISH APERITIF
- ¼ OZ. ST-GERMAIN
- 4 DROPS OF DR. ADAM ELMEGIRAB'S DANDELION & BURDOCK BITTERS
- 2 OZ. SODA WATER

Place all of the ingredients in a cocktail shaker, fill it two-thirds of the way with ice, and shake until chilled.

Strain over ice into the wineglass, garnish with the fresh dill, cucumber ribbon, and edible flower blossoms, and enjoy.

# Sgroppino Plagiato

*There's no better way to celebrate the miracle of homemade sorbet than this fizzy, bitter iteration of the beloved Italian cocktail.*

**GLASSWARE:** GOBLET

**GARNISH:** EDIBLE FLOWER BLOSSOM

**SCOOP OF TROPICAL FRUIT SORBET (SEE RECIPE)**

**1¾ OZ. SELECT APERITIVO**

**PROSECCO, TO TOP**

Place the scoop of sorbet in the goblet.

Pour the Select Aperitivo over the sorbet and top with prosecco.

Garnish with the edible flower blossom and serve with a spoon.

**TROPICAL FRUIT SORBET:** Place 3½ oz. water, 3½ oz. sugar, and ½ oz. fresh lemon juice in a saucepan and bring to a simmer, stirring until the sugar has dissolved. Add the seeds of 1 vanilla bean, 14 oz. mango puree, and 3½ oz. passion fruit puree and stir until combined. Freeze for 24 hours and let the mixture sit at room temperature for 5 or 10 minutes before serving. Churn the mixture in an ice cream maker if a smoother consistency is desired.

**SAGE & MINT AGAVE:** Place 9 oz. agave nectar, 2 ½ oz. water, 50 fresh mint leaves, and 8 fresh sage leaves in a blender and puree until smooth. Strain the mixture through cheesecloth before using or storing.

# Very Hungry Manzanilla

*A cheeky play on the famed children's book by Eric Carle,* The Very Hungry Caterpillar, *this very grown-up drink has plenty of depth, belying the green hue.*

**GLASSWARE:** COLLINS GLASS

**GARNISH:** PERFORATED SPRIG OF FRESH MINT, CANDY CATERPILLAR

- 1¼ **OZ. PLANTATION 3 STARS RUM**
- ½ **OZ. MANZANILLA SHERRY**
- ¾ **OZ. FRESH LIME JUICE**
- ½ **OZ. SAGE & MINT AGAVE (SEE RECIPE)**
- **SELTZER WATER, TO TOP**

Place all of the ingredients, except for the seltzer, in a cocktail shaker, fill it two-thirds of the way with ice, and shake until chilled.

Double strain over ice into the Collins glass and top with seltzer.

Garnish with the perforated sprig of mint and the candy caterpillar and enjoy.

# Sacred Lotus

*Tamarind's protean flavor—moving from tart to buttery to sweet as it passes over the tongue—makes this serve a certain palate awakener.*

**GLASSWARE:** WINEGLASS

**GARNISH:** CUCUMBER SLICE, FRESH BERRIES, LEMON WHEEL, ORANGE SLICE, FRESH MINT

**1 OZ. TAMARIND-INFUSED VODKA (SEE RECIPE)**

**1 OZ. ST-GERMAIN**

**PROSECCO, TO TOP**

Place the vodka and St-Germain in the wineglass, add ice, and top with prosecco.

Garnish with the cucumber slice, berries, lemon wheel, orange slice, and fresh mint and enjoy.

**TAMARIND-INFUSED VODKA:** Place ⅓ cup deseeded tamarind pulp and 4 cups vodka in a large mason jar and store in a cool, dark place for 1 week, shaking it daily. Strain before using or storing.

**UMEBOSHI POWDER:** Using a dehydrator on a setting for vegetables, spread pitted and pickled umeboshi plums on a tray and dehydrate for 3 days. This will produce a perfectly dry plum, which can then be ground into a powder.

**SUGAR SNAP PEA SYRUP:** Place ½ cup water in a saucepan and bring it to a boil. Add 1 lb. sugar and stir until it has dissolved. Remove the pan from heat and let the syrup cool. Stir in 5⅓ oz. sugar snap pea juice and use immediately or store in the refrigerator.

# Farm & Vine

*A globe-trotting cocktail that still manages to make you feel right at home.*

 **GLASSWARE:** ROCKS GLASS

**GARNISH:** SHISO LEAF, UMEBOSHI POWDER (SEE RECIPE)

| | |
|---|---|
| 1 | OZ. AQUAVIT |
| ¾ | OZ. MANZANILLA SHERRY |
| ½ | OZ. VERJUS |
| ¾ | OZ. FRESH LIME JUICE |
| ¾ | OZ. SUGAR SNAP PEA SYRUP (SEE RECIPE) |
| ½ | OZ. EGG WHITE |
| 1 | OZ. Q ELDERFLOWER TONIC |

Place all of the ingredients, except for the elderflower tonic, in a cocktail shaker and dry shake for 10 seconds.

Fill the cocktail shaker two-thirds of the way with ice and shake until chilled.

Add the elderflower tonic to the cocktail shaker, strain the cocktail into the rocks glass, and add a few ice cubes.

Garnish the cocktail with the shiso leaf and Umeboshi Powder and enjoy.

# Rose Blossom

*Don't be fooled by the pink glitter; there's a lot of depth here. The gin imparts a little punch; the Italicus brings earthy, herbal goodness; the elderflower cordial adds something fragrant; and the sparkling wine adds the refreshment you want in a spritz.*

**GLASSWARE:** COUPE

**GARNISH:** EDIBLE PINK GLITTER

| | |
|---|---|
| 2 | TEASPOONS TANQUERAY NO. TEN |
| 1¼ | OZ. ITALICUS ROSOLIO DI BERGAMOTTO |
| 2 | TEASPOONS BOTTLEGREEN ELDERFLOWER CORDIAL |
| 3 | DASHES OF PEYCHAUD'S BITTERS |
| | SPARKLING WINE, TO TOP |

Chill the coupe in the freezer.

Place all of the ingredients, except for the sparkling wine, in a mixing glass, fill it two-thirds of the way with ice, and stir until chilled.

Place a small block of ice in the chilled coupe and double strain the cocktail over it.

Top with sparkling wine, garnish with edible pink glitter, and enjoy.

# Fleur de Lis

*The verjus is the key to keeping the rich combination of Peychaud's and Cognac from overwhelming your stirring tastebuds.*

**GLASSWARE:** ROCKS GLASS

**GARNISH:** STRIP OF ORANGE PEEL

| | |
|---|---|
| 1 | OZ. PEYCHAUD'S BITTERS |
| ¾ | OZ. COGNAC |
| ¾ | OZ. VERJUS |
| ¼ | OZ. HONEY WATER (SEE RECIPE) |
| 2 | LEMON PEELS |
| | SPARKLING WINE, TO TOP |

Place all of the ingredients, except for the sparkling wine, in a mixing glass, fill it two-thirds of the way with ice, and stir until chilled.

Strain over a large ice cube into the rocks glass, top with sparkling wine, garnish with the strip of orange peel, and enjoy.

**HONEY WATER:** Place 1 cup wildflower honey and 1½ cups warm water in a mason jar, stir to combine, and let the mixture cool completely before using or storing.

# Yokota

*There's no wasted motion in this spritz—every element brings something significant to the table.*

**GLASSWARE:** WHITE WINEGLASS

**GARNISH:** NONE

| | |
|---|---|
| 1 | OZ. LUSTAU MOSCATEL SHERRY |
| 2 | BAR SPOONS FRESH LEMON JUICE |
| 2 | BAR SPOONS SIMPLE SYRUP (SEE RECIPE) |
| | CAVA, TO TOP |

Place all of the ingredients, except for the Cava, in a blender with crushed ice, pulse gently until the mixture is slushy, and pour it into the white wineglass.

Top with Cava, use a spoon to lift it and incorporate it into the slushy, and enjoy.

**SIMPLE SYRUP:** Place 1 cup sugar and 1 cup water in a saucepan and bring it to a boil, stirring to dissolve the sugar. Remove the pan from heat and let the syrup cool completely before using or storing.

# Deci's Roommate

*Made with a mix of rosé and brandy, this bright and bubbly cocktail is a good one to turn to if you're hosting a brunch that starts on the earlier side of things.*

**GLASSWARE:** ROCKS GLASS

**GARNISH:** FRESH MINT

| | |
|---|---|
| 1 | OZ. CALVADOS |
| ¾ | OZ. FRESH LIME JUICE |
| ½ | OZ. RICH SIMPLE SYRUP (SEE RECIPE) |
| 2 | OZ. SPARKLING ROSÉ |

Place the Calvados, lime juice, and syrup in a cocktail shaker, fill it two-thirds of the way with ice, and shake until chilled.

Pour the rosé into the shaker and then strain over ice into the rocks glass.

Garnish with fresh mint and enjoy.

**RICH SIMPLE SYRUP:** Place 2 cups sugar and 1 cup water in a saucepan and bring it to a boil, stirring to dissolve the sugar. Remove the pan from heat and let the syrup cool completely before using or storing.

# Americano

*The name of this drink is a nod to how Americans preferred to drink their vermouth back in the 1860s, though it wasn't until a couple decades later that the addition of soda water made its way into the official recipe. No matter what you call it, the combo of Campari, vermouth, and soda is refreshing, bitter, and a tad sweet in all the right ways.*

**GLASSWARE:** ROCKS GLASS

**GARNISH:** ORANGE SLICE

- **1 OZ. CAMPARI**
- **1 OZ. CINZANO 1757 VERMOUTH DI TORINO GI ROSSO**
- **SPLASH OF SODA WATER**

Fill the rocks glass with ice, add the Campari and vermouth, and stir until chilled.

Top with the soda water, garnish with the orange slice, and enjoy.

# Select Spritz

*Select Aperitivo claims to have started the whole spritz trend with this blend of classic liqueur with soda water and prosecco. More complex and more bitter than other Italian bitters, Select is perfect for a predinner drink in the summer.*

**GLASSWARE:** WHITE WINEGLASS

**GARNISH:** CASTELVETRANO OLIVE

3 OZ. PROSECCO

2 OZ. SELECT APERITIVO

1 OZ. SODA WATER

Fill the white wineglass with ice, add all of the ingredients, and gently stir.

Garnish with the olive and enjoy.

# Negroni Sbagliato

*Carpano Antica Formula is another good sweet vermouth option in this increasingly popular serve.*

**GLASSWARE:** WINEGLASS

**GARNISH:** LIME SLICE

| | |
|---|---|
| 1 | OZ. CAMPARI |
| 1 | OZ. CINZANO PROSECCO |
| 1 | OZ. CINZANO 1757 VERMOUTH DI TORINO GI ROSSO |

Fill the wineglass with ice, add all of the ingredients, and gently stir.

Garnish with the lime slice and enjoy.

# Sicilian Sbagliato

*Refreshing, but with enough citrus to dazzle your taste buds and hold your attention.*

**GLASSWARE:** HIGHBALL GLASS

**GARNISH:** EDIBLE FLOWER BLOSSOM

- ¾ OZ. LUXARDO BITTER BIANCO
- ¾ OZ. DOLIN BLANC VERMOUTH
- ½ OZ. LIMONCELLO
- 2 DASHES OF LEMON BITTERS
- 2½ OZ. PROSECCO
- ½ OZ. SAN PELLEGRINO

Place all of the ingredients, except for the prosecco and San Pellegrino, in a cocktail shaker, fill it two-thirds of the way with ice, and shake until chilled.

Strain over a large block of ice into the highball glass, top with the prosecco and San Pellegrino, and gently stir.

Garnish with the edible flower blossom and enjoy.

# Stazione

*If you're someone who loves a Gin & Tonic during cocktail hour, turn to this serve, which is a little sweeter and a bit more minty than a classic G & T.*

**GLASSWARE:** TUMBLER
**GARNISH:** LIME WEDGE

| | |
|---|---|
| 1 | OZ. STREGA |
| 1 | OZ. GIN |
| 4 | OZ. TONIC WATER |

Chill the tumbler in the freezer.

Fill the chilled tumbler with ice, add the Strega and gin, and slowly pour the tonic into the glass.

Garnish with the lime wedge and enjoy.

# Campari Seltz

*A signature spritz that shows just how simple making a really great cocktail can be.*

 **GLASSWARE:** TULIP GLASS
**GARNISH:** NONE

| | |
|---|---|
| **3 OZ. CAMPARI, CHILLED** | Chill the tulip glass in the freezer. |
| **SELTZER WATER, TO TOP** | Pour the Campari into the chilled glass, slowly pour seltzer into the glass, and enjoy. |

# Vermuttino

*Martini & Rossi makes a perfect not-too-sweet vermouth, and when mixed with soda water, it brightens, refreshes, and tickles your nostrils. This one is great on a late summer evening as you're waiting for the grill to warm up.*

**GLASSWARE:** HIGHBALL GLASS

**GARNISH:** LEMON TWIST

| | |
|---|---|
| 2 **OZ. MARTINI & ROSSI ROSSO SWEET VERMOUTH** | Fill the highball glass with ice, add the vermouth and soda water, and gently stir. |
| 3 **OZ. SODA WATER** | Garnish with the lemon twist and enjoy. |

# Diciotto

*Sweet, minty, fruity, and tart, this complex cocktail also makes for a great celebratory serve and a more-than-possible Mimosa stand-in at brunch.*

**GLASSWARE:** GOBLET

**GARNISH:** STRIP OF PINK GRAPEFRUIT PEEL

| | |
|---|---|
| 1 | OZ. STREGA |
| 1 | OZ. PINK GRAPEFRUIT JUICE |
| 2 | DASHES OF ANGOSTURA BITTERS |
| 1⅔ | OZ. CHAMPAGNE |

Place the Strega, grapefruit juice, and bitters in a cocktail shaker, fill it two-thirds of the way with ice, and shake until chilled.

Strain into the goblet and top with the Champagne.

Garnish with the strip of grapefruit peel and enjoy.

# Extra Sonic

*Hitting some vermouth with a double dose of bubbles and a touch of anise produces a memorable spritz.*

**GLASSWARE:** COLLINS GLASS

**GARNISH:** FRESH MINT

| | |
|---|---|
| 2 | OZ. COCCHI VERMOUTH DI TORINO EXTRA DRY |
| 3 | DROPS OF ABSINTHE |
| 2 | OZ. SODA WATER |
| 2 | OZ. TONIC WATER |

Fill the Collins glass with ice, add all of the ingredients, and gently stir.

Garnish with fresh mint and enjoy.

# Italicus Cup

*Italicus is citrusy, bitter, and floral, and when you combine it with grapefruit soda, a subtle sweetness enters the picture. Those qualities make this a dazzling aperitif, capable of transporting you to the Amalfi Coast, where Italicus hails from.*

**GLASSWARE:** HIGHBALL GLASS

**GARNISH:** GRAPEFRUIT OR ORANGE SLICE

1½ OZ. GRAPEFRUIT SODA

1 OZ. ITALICUS ROSOLIO DI BERGAMOTTO

Fill the highball glass with ice, add the ingredients, and gently stir.

Garnish with the grapefruit slice and enjoy.

# Broken Bicyclette

*Don't be put off by the name, Bicyclette fans—this is a wonderful summer sipper, sweet and effervescent without being overbearing.*

**GLASSWARE:** HIGHBALL GLASS

**GARNISH:** FRESH THYME

- 3 OZ. DRY WHITE WINE
- 1 OZ. PEACH NECTAR
- 2 OZ. SELECT APERITIVO
- 1 OZ. SODA WATER

Place the wine, peach nectar, and aperitivo in a cocktail shaker, fill it two-thirds of the way with ice, and shake until chilled.

Strain over ice into the highball glass, top with the soda water, and gently stir.

Garnish with fresh thyme and enjoy.

# Sour Cherry Spritz

*If pasta is on the menu, this cocktail should be as well—so long as you keep in mind that in terms of the spritz world, it sports a pretty high ABV.*

**GLASSWARE:** WINEGLASS

**GARNISH:** LUXARDO MARASCHINO CHERRY, SYRUP FROM LUXARDO MARASCHINO CHERRIES

- ¾ OZ. MARENDRY AMARENA WILD CHERRY APERITIVO
- ½ OZ. BORDIGA MARASCHINO LIQUEUR
- ½ OZ. VODKA
- SPLASH OF SODA WATER
- PROSECCO, TO TOP

Place the aperitivo, liqueur, and vodka in the wineglass, stir to combine, and add the soda water.

Add ice and top with prosecco.

Garnish with the maraschino cherry and syrup from the cherries and enjoy.

# Rosa Spritz

*A wonderful cocktail to introduce people to the fruity, spicy, and slightly bitter wonder that is Cocchi Americano Rosa.*

**GLASSWARE:** HIGHBALL GLASS

**GARNISH:** DEHYDRATED STRAWBERRY, FRESH BASIL

| | |
|---|---|
| 2 | OZ. COCCHI AMERICANO ROSA |
| 2 | OZ. PROSECCO |
| | SPARKLING WATER, TO TOP |

Chill the highball glass in the freezer.

Add ice to the chilled glass, add the Cocchi Americano Rosa and prosecco, and gently stir.

Top with sparkling water, garnish with the dehydrated strawberry and fresh basil, and enjoy.

# REFRESH

WHEN THE HEAT
STARTS TO BECOME
UNBEARABLE, IT'S
CRUCIAL TO SIT AND
RECHARGE WITH
A LIGHT, LONG,
AND EFFERVESCENT
DRINK—ALL OF WHICH
ARE SPECIALTIES OF
THE SPRITZ.

# Pacific Rhythms

*Midori's bright green hue, and its time as a key ingredient in a number of regrettable drinks mixed up during the 1980s means that many have negative associations with it. However, that stance is due for some revamping, as Suntory introduced a revised formula for the spirit in 2012. Now featuring two Japanese melon varieties and a drier profile, Midori is ready for a renaissance.*

**GLASSWARE:** COLLINS GLASS

**GARNISH:** FRESH MINT, LIME WHEEL, EDIBLE FLOWER

| | |
|---|---|
| | MATCHA POWDER, FOR THE RIM |
| | SUGAR, FOR THE RIM |
| 2 | CUCUMBER SLICES |
| 2 | OZ. BELUGA NOBLE VODKA |
| ½ | OZ. MIDORI |
| ½ | OZ. LUXARDO MARASCHINO LIQUEUR |
| ¾ | OZ. FRESH LEMON JUICE |
| ½ | OZ. SIMPLE SYRUP (SEE PAGE 34) |
| | FEVER-TREE SPARKLING LIME & YUZU, TO TOP |

Combine matcha powder and sugar in a small dish. Wet the rim of the Collins glass and coat it with mixture. Add ice to the rimmed glass.

Place all of the remaining ingredients, except the tonic water, in a cocktail shaker and muddle.

Add ice and shake until chilled.

Strain the cocktail into the rimmed glass and top with sparkling water.

Garnish with fresh mint, the lime wheel, and edible flower and enjoy.

# Pimm's Cup

*Don't think twice about mixing up a massive batch of this British classic if you've got guests for the weekend—is refreshing and revitalizing enough to carry your crew throughout.*

**GLASSWARE:** COLLINS GLASS

**GARNISH:** FRESH MINT

- 1 OZ. PIMM'S NO. 1
- 1 ORANGE SLICE
- 1 LEMON SLICE
- 1 CUCUMBER SLICE
- 1 STRAWBERRY, HULLED AND SLICED
- 2 OZ. LEMONADE
- 2½ OZ. GINGER ALE

Add ice to the Collins glass, pour in the Pimm's, and stir until chilled.

Add the orange, lemon, cucumber, and strawberry, top with the lemonade and ginger ale, and gently stir.

Garnish with fresh mint and enjoy.

# Formosa Fizz

*An agave-centered spin on the classic Clover Club cocktail, amping up the fizzy element with soda water.*

**GLASSWARE:** CHAMPAGNE FLUTE

**GARNISH:** FRESH RASPBERRIES

- 1½ OZ. SILVER TEQUILA
- ¾ OZ. FRESH LEMON JUICE
- ½ OZ. RASPBERRY SYRUP (SEE RECIPE)
- ½ OZ. EGG WHITE
- ¼ OZ. RICH SIMPLE SYRUP (SEE PAGE 37)
- 1½ OZ. SODA WATER, CHILLED

Place all of the ingredients, except for the soda water, in a cocktail shaker, fill it two-thirds of the way with ice, and shake until chilled and foamy.

Strain into the Champagne flute and top with the soda water.

Garnish with fresh raspberries and enjoy.

**RASPBERRY SYRUP:** Combine 500 grams raspberries and 500 grams sugar in a deep saucepan, then gently press down the mixture with the back of a fork. Let it macerate for 15 minutes, then add 500 ml water. Bring the mixture to just below a boil. Remove the pan from heat and let the syrup cool for 30 minutes. Strain the syrup through a fine-mesh sieve or cheesecloth before using or storing in the refrigerator.

# The Garden

*Gin mixes surprisingly well with a wide range of different vegetable juices. Here, fresh beet juice is the partner, creating an alarmingly pink cocktail with a rich, earthy flavor profile.*

**GLASSWARE:** TUMBLER

**GARNISH:** THIN SLICE OF BEET, EDIBLE ROSE PETALS

| | |
|---|---|
| 1½ | OZ. GIN |
| ½ | OZ. ROSE SYRUP (SEE RECIPE) |
| 1 | OZ. FRESH BEET JUICE |
| ½ | OZ. FRESH LEMON JUICE |
| 1½ TO 2 | OZ. Q TONIC WATER |

Place all of the ingredients in a cocktail shaker, fill it two-thirds of the way with ice, and shake until chilled.

Pour the contents of the shaker into the tumbler, garnish with the slice of beet and rose petals, and enjoy.

**ROSE SYRUP:** Place 1 cup rose water in a saucepan and bring to a boil. Add 1 cup sugar and stir until it has dissolved. Remove the pan from heat and let the syrup cool completely before using.

# Pink Sky

*Aperol, St-Germain, and a spicy shrub make this imaginative take on the Paloma a can't miss once the summer arrives.*

**GLASSWARE:** COLLINS GLASS

**GARNISH:** GRAPEFRUIT WHEEL, LIME WHEEL, DEHYDRATED GRAPEFRUIT CHIP

- 1½ OZ. TEQUILA
- 1 OZ. GRAPEFRUIT JUICE
- ¾ OZ. FRESH LIME JUICE
- ¼ OZ. APEROL
- ¼ OZ. ST-GERMAIN
- ¼ OZ. THAI PEPPER SHRUB (SEE RECIPE)
- FEVER-TREE LEMON TONIC WATER, TO TOP

Place all of the ingredients, except for the tonic, in the Collins glass, add ice, and stir until chilled.

Top with tonic, garnish with the grapefruit wheel, lime wheel, and dehydrated grapefruit chip, and enjoy.

**THAI PEPPER SHRUB:** Place 4 chopped Thai chile peppers, ¼ cup cane vinegar, and ¼ cup cane sugar in a saucepan and bring to a boil. Cook for 5 minutes, remove the pan from heat, and let the shrub cool completely. Strain before using or storing.

# Basilico

*The basil lends a pleasant touch of anise, while the lemon thyme allows the vermouth to articulate a sweet, citric note that complements the gin.*

**GLASSWARE:** CHAMPAGNE FLUTE

**GARNISH:** FRESH BASIL

| | |
|---|---|
| 4 | FRESH BASIL LEAVES |
| 1 | OZ. TANQUERAY NO. TEN |
| 1 | OZ. LEMON THYME–INFUSED VERMOUTH (SEE RECIPE) |
| | FEVER-TREE MEDITERRANEAN TONIC WATER, TO TOP |

Slap the basil leaves and add them to a cocktail shaker. Fill it two-thirds of the way with ice, add the gin and vermouth, and shake until chilled.

Double strain into the Champagne flute, add a few ice cubes, and top with tonic.

Garnish with additional fresh basil and enjoy.

**LEMON THYME–INFUSED VERMOUTH:** Place 3 sprigs of fresh lemon thyme in a 700 ml bottle of dry vermouth and steep for 24 hours. Remove the sprigs of lemon thyme before using or storing.

# Lady in Red

*Another cocktail inspired by the Negroni Sbagliato, this is irresistibly tart and floral and features a fruity finish.*

**GLASSWARE:** COUPE

**GARNISH:** NONE

- ¾ OZ. LONDON DRY GIN
- ½ OZ. CAMPARI
- ¼ OZ. STRAWBERRY VINEGAR (SEE RECIPE)
- 2 OZ. SPARKLING WINE

Place all of the ingredients in a mixing glass, fill it two-thirds of the way with ice, and gently stir until chilled.

Strain over a large ice cube into the coupe and enjoy.

**STRAWBERRY VINEGAR:** Place 10½ oz. fresh strawberries, 26 oz. apple cider vinegar, 2 sliced lemons, 1 teaspoon grenadine, and 1½ oz. Simple Syrup (see page 34) in a mason jar and let the mixture steep for 3 days. Strain, taste to see if it is sweet enough, and add more Simple Syrup if necessary.

# High C Spritz

*Think of this as an opera for your palate and potentially a pretty good choice to warm up your vocal cords before taking your turn on karaoke night.*

**GLASSWARE:** CHAMPAGNE FLUTE

**GARNISH:** 3 KALAMATA OLIVES

- 1 OZ. OLIVE LEAF–INFUSED GIN (SEE RECIPE)
- 2 TEASPOONS ACQUA DI CEDRO NARDINI
- 2 TEASPOONS DRY VERMOUTH
- ½ TEASPOON SUZE
- 2 OZ. THREE CENTS GENTLEMEN'S SODA

Build the cocktail in the Champagne flute, adding the ingredients in the order they are listed. Gently stir.

Garnish with the Kalamata olives and enjoy.

**OLIVE LEAF–INFUSED GIN:** Place a 750 ml bottle of Hendrick's Orbium Gin and 4 oz. dried olive leaves in a mason jar and store in a cool, dark place for 5 days. Strain before using or storing.

# I Wish I Was in New Orleans

*For those that love New Orleans, each year will inevitably contain a few evenings where one sits with a cocktail and pines for the Crescent City.*

**GLASSWARE:** CHAMPAGNE FLUTE

**GARNISH:** STRIP OF LEMON PEEL

| | |
|---|---|
| ⅔ | **OZ. HAVANA CLUB 7 YEAR RUM** |
| ⅓ | **OZ. ELDERFLOWER LIQUEUR** |
| 1¼ | **TEASPOONS FRESH LIME JUICE** |
| 2 | **DASHES OF PEYCHAUD'S BITTERS** |
| | **CHAMPAGNE, TO TOP** |

Place all of the ingredients, except for the Champagne, in a cocktail shaker, fill it two-thirds of the way with ice, and shake until chilled.

Strain the cocktail into the Champagne flute and top with Champagne.

Garnish with the strip of lemon peel and enjoy.

# El Cuco

*The addition of effervescence keys this refreshing take on the Navy Grog, a tiki classic.*

**GLASSWARE:** ROCKS GLASS

**GARNISH:** LIME WEDGE, SPRIG OF MINT

- 1 OZ. APPLETON ESTATE SIGNATURE BLEND RUM
- ½ OZ. HAMILTON GUYANA 86 RUM
- ½ OZ. CAÑA BRAVA 7 YEAR RUM
- ½ OZ. EL DORADO 3 YEAR RUM
- ¾ OZ. FRESH LIME JUICE
- ¾ OZ. GRAPEFRUIT JUICE
- ¾ OZ. HONEY & GINGER SYRUP (SEE RECIPE)
- SELTZER WATER, TO TOP

Place all of the ingredients, except for the seltzer, in a cocktail shaker, fill it two-thirds of the way with ice, and shake until chilled.

Fill the rocks glass with crushed ice and strain the cocktail over it.

Top the cocktail with seltzer, garnish it with the lime wedge and fresh mint, and enjoy.

**HONEY & GINGER SYRUP:** Place 1 cup water, 1 cup honey, and a chopped 2-inch piece of fresh ginger in a saucepan and bring to a boil. Cook for 4 minutes, remove the pan from heat, and let the syrup cool completely. Strain before using or storing.

# Stranger Things

*The fruitiness supplied by the strawberry-laced vodka and passion fruit puree makes the nice, dry finish provided by the prosecco essential to the drink.*

**GLASSWARE:** LIGHTBULB GLASS OR CHAMPAGNE FLUTE

**GARNISH:** RASPBERRY

- 1⅜ OZ. STRAWBERRY TEA–INFUSED VODKA (SEE RECIPE)
- 1⅜ OZ. PASSION FRUIT PUREE
- ¾ OZ. SIMPLE SYRUP (SEE PAGE 34)
- PROSECCO, TO TOP

Place the vodka, passion fruit puree, and syrup in a cocktail shaker, fill it two-thirds of the way with ice, and shake until chilled.

Double strain into a lightbulb glass or Champagne flute and top with prosecco.

Garnish with the raspberry and enjoy.

**STRAWBERRY TEA–INFUSED VODKA:** Place 3 bags of strawberry tea and a 750 ml bottle of vodka in a mason jar, shake vigorously, and steep for 24 hours. Remove the tea bags before using or storing.

# Hugo

*Fiorente's elderflower liqueur is on the less sweet side of the options out there, and thus is a great match for prosecco and seltzer.*

**GLASSWARE:** WINEGLASS

**GARNISH:** FRESH MINT

1 OZ. FIORENTE ELDERFLOWER LIQUEUR

3 OZ. PROSECCO

2 OZ. SELTZER

Fill the wineglass with ice, add all of the ingredients, and gently stir to combine.

Slap the fresh mint, garnish the cocktail with it, and enjoy.

# Sideways

*Tart, herbal, and subtly sweet, this is a startlingly complex cocktail for something that is also undeniably elegant.*

**GLASSWARE:** COLLINS GLASS

**GARNISH:** FRESH MINT

| | |
|---|---|
| ¾ | OZ. SIMPLE SYRUP (SEE PAGE 34) |
| 10 | FRESH MINT LEAVES |
| 2½ | OZ. GRAPPA NONINO MONOVITIGNO MERLOT |
| 1 | OZ. FRESH LIME JUICE |
| | SODA WATER, TO TOP |

Place the lime juice and syrup in the Collins glass and muddle.

Add ice and the grappa, top with soda water, and gently stir.

Garnish with additional mint and enjoy.

# Fruity Bag

*This spritz has an inventive means of working wine into the mix, slipping it into the syrup.*

**GLASSWARE:** HIGHBALL GLASS

**GARNISH:** STRAWBERRY

- 1⅓ OZ. VODKA
- ⅔ OZ. ROSÉ & STRAWBERRY SYRUP (SEE RECIPE)
- BLOOD ORANGE TONIC WATER, TO TOP

Chill the highball glass in the freezer.

Place the vodka and syrup in a mixing glass, fill it two-thirds of the way with ice, and stir until chilled.

Strain over ice into the chilled highball glass.

Garnish with the strawberry and serve.

**ROSÉ & STRAWBERRY SYRUP:** Place 15 strawberries, 1 cup rosé, and 1 cup sugar in a saucepan and bring to a boil, stirring to dissolve the sugar. Remove the pan from heat and let the syrup cool completely. Strain before using or storing.

# St. Kilda

*The freshness of the watermelon shrub and a salted rim help this spritz taste like summer in a glass.*

**GLASSWARE:** HIGHBALL GLASS

**GARNISH:** WATERMELON WEDGE

|  | |
|---|---|
|  | **BLACK LAVA SALT, FOR THE RIM** |
| 1 | **OZ. SILVER TEQUILA** |
| ⅓ | **OZ. FRESH LIME JUICE** |
| ⅔ | **OZ. WATERMELON SHRUB (SEE RECIPE)** |
|  | **FEVER-TREE SPARKLING PINK GRAPEFRUIT, TO TOP** |

Wet the rim of the highball glass and rim half of it with black lava salt.

Fill the rimmed glass with ice, add the tequila, lime juice, and shrub, and stir until chilled.

Top with grapefruit soda, garnish with the watermelon wedge, and enjoy.

**WATERMELON SHRUB:** Combine 34 oz. fresh watermelon juice, 1¼ lbs. sugar, and 5 oz. apple cider vinegar in a saucepan and bring to a simmer, stirring to dissolve the sugar. Simmer for 5 minutes, remove the pan from heat, and let the shrub cool completely before using or storing.

**RASPBERRY CORDIAL:** Place ½ lb. fresh raspberries, 4 oz. caster (superfine) sugar, and the zest of 1 lime in a small saucepan and bring to a simmer over medium-low heat, stirring to dissolve the sugar and mashing the berries. Simmer for 20 minutes, remove the pan from heat, and let the mixture cool completely. Stir in the juice of 1 lime, double strain the cordial into a mason jar, and use as desired.

# Purple Rain

*A spritz that is brimming with lively, bold, and fruity flavors, and features a pleasant balance of sweet and sour aromas.*

**GLASSWARE:** COLLINS GLASS

**GARNISH:** DEHYDRATED ORANGE WHEEL

| | |
|---|---|
| 1 | OZ. VODKA |
| 1 | OZ. ALIZÉ GOLD PASSION |
| 1 | OZ. SIMPLE SYRUP (SEE PAGE 34) |
| 1 | OZ. FRESH LEMON JUICE |
| ½ | OZ. RASPBERRY CORDIAL (SEE RECIPE) |
| | SODA WATER, TO TOP |

Chill the Collins glass in the freezer.

Place all of the ingredients, except for the soda water, in a cocktail shaker, fill it two-thirds of the way with ice, and shake until chilled.

Fill the chilled Collins glass with crushed ice and double strain the cocktail over it.

Top with soda water, garnish with the dehydrated orange wheel, and enjoy.

# Nami Spritz

*Sake and aloe vera juice may seem like unorthodox cocktail ingredients, but once you take a few sips of this smooth-tasting spritz, you'll be wondering why they aren't showing up more.*

**GLASSWARE:** HIGHBALL GLASS

**GARNISH:** LEMON WEDGE

| | |
|---|---|
| 1 | OZ. SAKE |
| ½ | OZ. LILLET BLANC |
| 3 | OZ. ALOE VERA JUICE |
| | SPARKLING WATER, TO TOP |

Fill the highball glass with ice and build the cocktail in it, adding the ingredients in the order they are listed.

Gently stir, garnish with the lemon wedge, and enjoy.

**ROSEMARY SYRUP:** Place 1 cup sugar, 1 cup water, and 4 sprigs of fresh rosemary in a small saucepan and simmer the mixture for 10 to 15 minutes, stirring occasionally. Remove from the pan from heat, strain, and let the syrup cool before using or storing.

# Summer Garden No. 1

*The subtle flavor of watermelon cries out for bold counterparts, a box ticked by the piney rosemary and spicy ginger beer here. Try to find a grenache rosé, as they tend to carry a fruity, floral profile that will shine in this cocktail.*

**GLASSWARE:** HIGHBALL GLASS

**GARNISH:** FRESH ROSEMARY

- 1⅓ OZ. DRY ROSÉ
- ⅔ OZ. FRESH LIME JUICE
- 1⅓ OZ. WATERMELON JUICE
- ⅔ OZ. ROSEMARY SYRUP (SEE RECIPE)
- GINGER BEER, TO TOP

Chill the highball glass in the freezer.

Place all of the ingredients, except for the ginger beer, in a cocktail shaker, fill it two-thirds of the way with ice, and shake until chilled.

Strain over ice into the chilled highball glass and top with ginger beer.

Garnish with fresh rosemary and enjoy.

# Cucumber & Rosé Highball

*Cocktails are a great spot to make use of sweet rosés, as they open up a number of potential paths to the desired result.*

**GLASSWARE:** HIGHBALL GLASS

**GARNISH:** CUCUMBER SLICE

- ½ OZ. SWEET ROSÉ
- 1⅔ OZ. LONDON DRY GIN
- ⅔ OZ. FRESH LEMON JUICE
- ½ OZ. CUCUMBER SYRUP (SEE RECIPE)
- FEVER-TREE ELDERFLOWER TONIC WATER, TO TOP

Chill the highball glass in the freezer.

Place all of the ingredients, except for the tonic water, in a cocktail shaker, fill it two-thirds of the way with ice, and shake until chilled.

Strain over ice into the chilled highball glass and top with tonic water.

Garnish with the cucumber slice and enjoy.

**CUCUMBER SYRUP:** Place the peels of 2 cucumbers, 1¼ cups water, and 1½ cups sugar in a saucepan and bring to a boil, stirring to dissolve the sugar. Remove the pan from heat and let the syrup cool completely. Strain before using or storing.

**STRAWBERRY-INFUSED VODKA:** Place 6⅔ oz. vodka and 10 halved strawberries in a mason jar, seal it, and store it in a cool, dark place. Let the mixture steep for 3 days, or until the flavor is to your liking. Strain before using or storing.

**BASIL SYRUP:** Place 1¼ cups water and 1½ cups sugar in a saucepan and bring to a boil, stirring to dissolve the sugar. Remove the pan from heat, add 20 fresh basil leaves, and let the syrup cool completely. Strain before using or storing.

# Floating Leaf

*The pairing of strawberry and basil is starting to pop up everywhere in the artisanal world, and as you'll see from the Floating Leaf, that's a grand thing.*

**GLASSWARE:** COUPE

**GARNISH:** FRESH BASIL

- 1⅓ OZ. STRAWBERRY-INFUSED VODKA (SEE RECIPE)
- ⅔ OZ. FRESH LEMON JUICE
- ½ OZ. BASIL SYRUP (SEE RECIPE)
- 2 OZ. SPARKLING ROSÉ

Chill the coupe in the freezer.

Place all of the ingredients, except for the rosé, in a cocktail shaker, fill it two-thirds of the way with ice, and shake until chilled.

Strain into the chilled coupe and top with the rosé.

Garnish with fresh basil and enjoy.

# Pink Strawberry Rosé

*The dry character of the gin is essential to balance out all of the berry notes in this serve.*

 **GLASSWARE:** HIGHBALL GLASS

**GARNISH:** LIME WEDGE

- ¾ OZ. GIN
- ⅓ OZ. FRESH LEMON JUICE
- ½ OZ. STRAWBERRY SYRUP (SEE RECIPE)
- DASH OF ORANGE BITTERS
- 3⅓ OZ. SPARKLING ROSÉ

Chill the highball glass in the freezer.

Place all of the ingredients, except for the sparkling rosé, in a cocktail shaker, fill it two-thirds of the way with ice, and shake until chilled.

Strain over ice into the chilled highball glass and top with the sparkling rosé.

Garnish with the lime wedge and enjoy.

**STRAWBERRY SYRUP:** Place 15 halved strawberries, 1¼ cup water, and 1 cup sugar in a saucepan and bring to a boil, stirring to dissolve the sugar. Remove the pan from heat and let the syrup cool completely. Strain before using or storing.

# RELAX

A LARGE PART OF BEING AT YOUR BEST IS ALLOWING YOURSELF TO TAKE A STEP BACK AND RECHARGE YOUR BATTERY. LIGHT AND LOW-ABV, THE SPRITZ IS A PERFECT PARTNER FOR THOSE MOMENTS WHERE RELAXATION IS THE PRIORITY.

# Paloma

*Thanks to the double dose of grapefruit and its easy-drinking nature, the popularity of the Paloma has surged over the last decade, putting it neck and neck with the king of agave-based cocktails, the Margarita.*

**GLASSWARE:** COLLINS GLASS

**GARNISH:** GRAPEFRUIT WEDGE, FRESH ROSEMARY

SALT, FOR THE RIM

2 OZ. TEQUILA

1 OZ. GRAPEFRUIT JUICE

½ OZ. FRESH LIME JUICE

PINK GRAPEFRUIT SODA, TO TOP

Wet the rim of the Collins glass and rim it with salt.

Fill the Collins glass with ice, add the tequila, grapefruit juice, and lime juice, and stir until chilled.

Top with grapefruit soda, gently stir, garnish with the grapefruit wedge and fresh rosemary, and enjoy.

# Mimosa

*This brunch classic brightens any environment it shows up in, proving that even in the cocktail world, it's the simple things that provide the most enjoyment.*

**GLASSWARE:** CHAMPAGNE FLUTE
**GARNISH:** NONE

3 OZ. ORANGE JUICE

3 OZ. CHAMPAGNE

Place the orange juice in the Champagne flute, top with the Champagne, and enjoy.

# Bellini

*If you prefer drinks that are a bit more inclined toward sweetness, swap the Champagne out for prosecco.*

**GLASSWARE:** CHAMPAGNE FLUTE

**GARNISH:** NONE

| 2 | OZ. PEACH NECTAR |
| ¼ | OZ. FRESH LEMON JUICE |
| | CHAMPAGNE, TO TOP |

Place the peach nectar and lemon juice in a cocktail shaker, fill it two-thirds of the way with ice, and shake until chilled.

Strain into the Champagne flute, top with Champagne, and enjoy.

# Berries & Bubbles

*Make sure you source the raspberries from a trusted place, at the height of their season, as it will make a massive difference in this straightforward spritz.*

**GLASSWARE:** COUPE

**GARNISH:** EDIBLE FLOWER BLOSSOMS OR FRESH RASPBERRY

| | |
|---|---|
| 3 TO 4 | FRESH RASPBERRIES |
| 1½ | OZ. VODKA OR GIN |
| ½ | OZ. SIMPLE SYRUP (SEE PAGE 34) |
| ½ | OZ. FRESH LEMON JUICE |
| 1½ | OZ. CHAMPAGNE OR SPARKLING ROSÉ |

Chill the coupe in the freezer.

Place all of the ingredients, except for the Champagne, in a cocktail shaker, fill it two-thirds of the way with ice, and shake until chilled.

Double strain the cocktail into the chilled coupe.

Top with the Champagne, garnish with edible flower blossoms or a raspberry, and enjoy.

# Flash Gordon

*While craft gins have flooded the market over the last two decades, Gordon's remains one of the best options for cocktails, as evidenced by its status as the go-to for some of the world's best bartenders.*

**GLASSWARE:** HIGHBALL GLASS

**GARNISH:** NONE

- 1⅓ OZ. GORDON'S LONDON DRY GIN
- ½ OZ. FRESH LEMON JUICE
- 1 BAR SPOON SIMPLE SYRUP (SEE PAGE 34)
- 1 OZ. MILK
- CLUB SODA, TO TOP

Place all of the ingredients, except for the club soda, in a cocktail shaker, fill it two-thirds of the way with ice, and shake until chilled.

Strain over ice into the Collins glass, top with club soda, stirring the drink vigorously with a bar spoon as you pour, and enjoy.

# Fruits of the Monastic Life

*Assuming that you can track down a bottle of Chartreuse—the monks who produce it cut back on production in 2023—you'll see that it's a spritz standout, able to take the flavor in a number of directions.*

**GLASSWARE:** HIGHBALL GLASS

**GARNISH:** NONE

| | |
|---|---|
| 1 | BAR SPOON CASTER (SUPERFINE) SUGAR |
| | HANDFUL OF FRESH SPEARMINT |
| 1 | LIME WEDGE |
| 1 | OZ. BACARDÍ RUM |
| ⅔ | OZ. GREEN CHARTREUSE |
| | CLUB SODA, TO TOP |

Place the sugar and spearmint in the highball glass and muddle.

Squeeze the juice from the lime wedge into the glass, remove the lime pulp, discard it, and place the spent lime wedge in the glass.

Add the rum, Chartreuse, and cracked ice to the glass and top with club soda.

Stir until chilled and enjoy.

# Island Hopper

*The grassy, vegetal qualities of rhum agricole make it a good option in a spritz, where one typically wants refreshment rather than sweetness.*

**GLASSWARE:** COLLINS GLASS

**GARNISH:** PINEAPPLE LEAVES, DEHYDRATED LIME WHEEL

- 1½ OZ. RHUM AGRICOLE
- ½ OZ. HIBISCUS SYRUP (SEE RECIPE)
- ½ OZ. FRESH LEMON JUICE
- ¾ OZ. PINEAPPLE JUICE
- 2 OZ. GINGER BEER

Place all of the ingredients, except the ginger beer, in a cocktail shaker, fill it two-thirds of the way with ice, and shake until chilled.

Place the ginger beer in the Collins glass, strain the cocktail into the glass, and fill it with crushed ice.

Garnish the cocktail with the pineapple leaves and dehydrated lime wheel and enjoy.

**HIBISCUS SYRUP:** Place 1 teaspoon loose-leaf hibiscus tea in 1 cup Simple Syrup (see page 34) and steep for 10 days. Strain before using or storing in the refrigerator.

# Cherry Valance

*If you prefer a little bit more zip here, swap the ginger ale out for your favorite ginger beer.*

**GLASSWARE:** COLLINS GLASS

**GARNISH:** 2 FRESH SAGE LEAVES, FRESH BERRY OR GRIOTTINE

| | |
|---|---|
| 1¾ | OZ. VODKA |
| 1¾ | TEASPOONS SYRUP FROM A JAR OF GRIOTTINES |
| ½ | OZ. FRESH LIME JUICE |
| | FEVER-TREE GINGER ALE, TO TOP |

Place the vodka, syrup, and lime juice in the highball glass and fill it with ice. Stir for a few seconds.

Top with ginger ale and gently stir.

Garnish with the fresh sage and either a berry or a Griottine and enjoy.

# Rossini

*Named after nineteenth-century Italian composer Gioachino Rossini, this Bellini offshoot is simple to make, easy to drink, and able to work as well in the early evening as it is at a morning brunch.*

**GLASSWARE:** CHAMPAGNE FLUTE

**GARNISH:** FRESH STRAWBERRY

| | |
|---|---|
| 4 | FRESH STRAWBERRIES |
| 1 | TEASPOON CASTER (SUPERFINE) SUGAR |
| ½ | OZ. FRESH LEMON JUICE |
| 4 | OZ. PROSECCO |

Place the strawberries, sugar, and lemon juice in a cocktail shaker and muddle.

Add crushed ice to the shaker and shake until chilled.

Strain into the Champagne flute, top with the prosecco, and gently stir.

Garnish with an additional strawberry and enjoy.

# Aroma

*This spritz is both sweet and very tart, thanks to the limoncello and grapefruit juice, but the addition of Angostura bitters helps temper both of these.*

**GLASSWARE:** ROCKS GLASS

**GARNISH:** FRESH MINT

| | |
|---|---|
| 2 | OZ. LIMONCELLO |
| 1 | OZ. GRAPEFRUIT JUICE |
| 2 TO 3 | DASHES OF ANGOSTURA BITTERS |
| 3 | OZ. TONIC WATER |

Place the limoncello, grapefruit juice, and bitters in a mixing glass, fill it two-thirds of the way with ice, and stir until chilled.

Strain over ice into the rocks glass and top with the tonic water.

Garnish with fresh mint and enjoy.

# Distant Call

*This low-ABV drink is a sweet-tart thirst-quencher that goes really well with a hot summer day. Consider this when you're looking for a long, after-lunch drink out on a patio.*

**GLASSWARE:** WHITE WINEGLASS

**GARNISH:** STRIP OF LEMON PEEL

1½ OZ. DISARONNO ORIGINALE

SQUEEZE OF FRESH LEMON JUICE

CLUB SODA, TO TOP

Fill the wineglass with ice, add the Disaronno and lemon juice, and top with club soda.

Gently stir, garnish with the strip of lemon peel, and enjoy.

# Veruschka

*The vibrant red color lends this spritz a seductive quality, making it a great choice to start off a date.*

 **GLASSWARE:** CHAMPAGNE FLUTE

**GARNISH:** ROSE PETAL

1¼ OZ. FRESH POMEGRANATE PUREE

PROSECCO, TO TOP

SPLASH OF VODKA

Place the pomegranate puree in the Champagne flute and top with prosecco.

Add the vodka, garnish with the rose petal, and enjoy.

# Beverly Interpretation

*Bitter, sweet, and citrusy, Chinotto is at last starting to win fans outside of Italy, where it is beloved. Let this spritz serve as your introduction.*

**GLASSWARE:** CHAMPAGNE FLUTE

**GARNISH:** EDIBLE GREEN LEAF

- 1⅔ OZ. ITALICUS ROSOLIO DI BERGAMOTTO
- ½ OZ. FRESH PINK GRAPEFRUIT JUICE
- 5 OZ. CHINOTTO

Place all of the ingredients in a mixing glass, fill it two-thirds of the way with ice, and stir until chilled.

Strain into the Champagne flute, garnish with the green leaf, and enjoy.

# Mi-Và

*This drink is a good place to turn when you're entertaining and looking for something eye-catching to serve alongside a rich appetizer.*

**GLASSWARE:** HIGHBALL GLASS

**GARNISH:** PINK GRAPEFRUIT SLICE

| | |
|---|---|
| 1 | OZ. GIN |
| 1 | OZ. CAMPARI |
| ⅓ | OZ. SWEET & SOUR (SEE RECIPE) |
| | GRAPEFRUIT TONIC WATER, TO TOP |

Place the gin, Campari, and Sweet & Sour in a mixing glass, fill it two-thirds of the way with ice, and stir until chilled.

Strain over a large ice cube into the highball glass and top with tonic.

Garnish with the grapefruit slice and enjoy.

**SWEET & SOUR:** Place 2 oz. fresh lemon juice, 4 oz. fresh lime juice, and 6 oz. Rich Simple Syrup (see page 37) in a mason jar, seal it, and shake until combined. Use immediately or store in the refrigerator.

# The Marleybone Crush

*A fresh, punch-like drink that is packed with herbal undertones and a spice.*

**GLASSWARE:** HIGHBALL GLASS

**GARNISH:** SHAVED FRESH GINGER, 3 RASPBERRIES, FRESH MINT

- 1¾ OZ. GIN
- 1¼ OZ. CRANBERRY JUICE
- ½ OZ. FRESH LIME JUICE
- SPARKLING CIDER, TO TOP

Place all of the ingredients, except for the sparkling cider, in a cocktail shaker, fill it two-thirds of the way with ice, and shake until chilled.

Strain over ice into the highball glass and top with sparkling cider.

Garnish with the ginger, raspberries, and fresh mint and enjoy.

# Running Up That Hill

*When you've had one of those days, mix up one of these and hit reset.*

**GLASSWARE:** WINEGLASS

**GARNISH:** GRAPEFRUIT SLICE, FRESH ROSEMARY

- 1½ OZ. SILVER TEQUILA
- ¾ OZ. CAMPARI
- ½ OZ. FRESH LIME JUICE
- ½ OZ. FRESH RUBY RED GRAPEFRUIT JUICE
- ½ OZ. SIMPLE SYRUP (SEE PAGE 34)
- TOPO CHICO, TO TOP

Place all of the ingredients, except for the Topo Chico, in a cocktail shaker, fill it two-thirds of the way with ice, and shake until chilled.

Strain over ice into the wineglass and top with Topo Chico.

Garnish with the grapefruit slice and fresh rosemary and enjoy.

# Kissed by a Rose

*Smoky, tropical, and sour, this spritz has a surprising complexity thanks to the Scotch and infused rosé.*

**GLASSWARE:** HIGHBALL GLASS

**GARNISH:** PASSION FRUIT WEDGE

- 1 OZ. PASSION FRUIT ROSÉ (SEE RECIPE)
- 1⅓ OZ. BLENDED SCOTCH WHISKY
- ⅓ OZ. FRESH LEMON JUICE
- ⅓ OZ. RICH SIMPLE SYRUP
- SODA WATER, TO TOP

Place all of the ingredients, except for the soda water, in a cocktail shaker, fill it two-thirds of the way with ice, and shake until chilled.

Strain over ice into the highball glass and top with soda water.

Garnish with the passion fruit wedge and enjoy.

**PASSION FRUIT ROSÉ:** Place 3 sliced passion fruits and 10 oz. rosé in a vacuum bag, seal it, and sous vide at 140°F for 2 hours. Strain into a mason jar and let the infused rosé cool completely before using or storing.

# Mining for Gold

*The garnish of gold leaf is not there to exaggerate the luxurious nature of this serve, but celebrate it.*

 **GLASSWARE:** COLLINS GLASS

**GARNISH:** EDIBLE GOLD LEAF

- 1½ OZ. LIMONCELLO
- ½ OZ. VODKA
- 1 OZ. FRESH LEMON JUICE
- ½ OZ. SIMPLE SYRUP (SEE PAGE 34)
- SAN PELLEGRINO LIMONATA, TO TOP

Chill the Collins glass in the freezer.

Place all of the ingredients, except for the Limonata, in a cocktail shaker and dry shake for 10 seconds.

Add ice and shake until chilled.

Strain the cocktail into the chilled Collins glass and slowly pour in Limonata.

Garnish with gold leaf and enjoy.

# Gintarito

*Just be aware: it will be difficult to stop at one of these. Also, don't hesitate to experiment with different gins until you find the one that makes this perfect for you.*

**GLASSWARE:** HIGHBALL GLASS

**GARNISH:** DEHYDRATED ORANGE SLICE

- 1½ OZ. GIN
- ½ OZ. FRESH ORANGE JUICE
- ½ OZ. FRESH LIME JUICE
- ½ OZ. FRESH LEMON JUICE
- ½ OZ. VANILLA SYRUP (SEE RECIPE)
- GRAPEFRUIT SODA, TO TOP

Fill the highball glass with ice, add all of the ingredients, except for the soda, to the glass and gently stir.

Top with grapefruit soda, garnish with the dehydrated orange slice, and enjoy.

**VANILLA SYRUP:** Place 1 cup water in a small saucepan and bring it to a boil. Add 2 cups sugar and stir until it has dissolved. Remove the pan from heat. Halve 1 vanilla bean and scrape the seeds into the syrup. Cut the vanilla bean pod into thirds and add the pieces to the syrup. Stir to combine, cover the pan, and let the mixture sit at room temperature for 12 hours. Strain the syrup through cheesecloth before using or storing.

# Mind Games

*When shopping for apricot liqueurs, seek out Rothman & Winter's offering, as it has the lightness you want in a spritz.*

**GLASSWARE:** HIGHBALL GLASS

**GARNISH:** DEHYDRATED BLOOD ORANGE WHEEL, MARASCHINO CHERRY

- 1 OZ. LONDON DRY GIN
- ⅔ OZ. APRICOT LIQUEUR
- ⅔ OZ. FRESH LEMON JUICE
- ⅔ OZ. SIMPLE SYRUP (SEE PAGE 34)
- 3½ OZ. SODA WATER

Place all of the ingredients, except for the soda water, in a cocktail shaker, fill it two-thirds of the way with ice, and shake until chilled.

Pour the soda water into the highball glass, strain the cocktail into the glass, and add ice.

Garnish with the dehydrated blood orange wheel and maraschino cherry and enjoy.

# Piscomelo

*For those wondering, supreming citrus involves carefully removing the delicate pulp from the chewy membrane.*

**GLASSWARE:** ROCKS GLASS

**GARNISH:** GRAPEFRUIT WEDGE

| | |
|---|---|
| 2 | GRAPEFRUITS, SUPREMED |
| 2 | LEMON WEDGES |
| 1 | OZ. PISCO |
| ½ | OZ. AGAVE NECTAR |
| | GRAPEFRUIT SODA, TO TOP |

Place the grapefruit and lemon wedges in the rocks glass and muddle.

Add the pisco and agave nectar and stir until chilled.

Top with soda, garnish with the grapefruit wedge, and enjoy.

# Tea Time with Charley

*Pay attention any time St-Germain appears in a cocktail, as it signals that something complex and impeccably balanced has been authored.*

**GLASSWARE:** WINEGLASS

**GARNISH:** ORANGE TWIST

- 2 OZ. GIN
- 1 OZ. ST-GERMAIN
- 1 OZ. ORANGE JUICE
- ½ OZ. FRESH LIME JUICE
- 1 OZ. SPARKLING WINE

Place all of the ingredients, except for the sparkling wine, in a cocktail shaker, fill it two-thirds of the way with ice, and shake until chilled.

Strain over ice into the wineglass and top with the sparkling wine.

Garnish with the orange twist and enjoy.

# Raspberry Beret

*The soda water enhances everything here, providing irresistible effervescence, and brightening all of the other flavors present.*

**GLASSWARE:** HIGHBALL GLASS

**GARNISH:** LIME WEDGE, FRESH MINT

| | |
|---|---|
| 4 | RASPBERRIES |
| 1 | OZ. ROSÉ |
| 1 | OZ. VODKA |
| ¾ | OZ. FRESH LIME JUICE |
| ½ | OZ. RICH SIMPLE SYRUP (SEE PAGE 37) |
| 1⅔ | OZ. SODA WATER |

Place all of the ingredients, except for the soda water, in a cocktail shaker, fill it two-thirds of the way with ice, and shake until chilled.

Double strain over ice into the highball glass and top with the soda water.

Garnish with the lime wedge and fresh mint and enjoy.

# Sunlit Horizon

*Fruity with tart notes of rhubarb, Aperol is a wonderful match for sparkling rosé.*

 **GLASSWARE:** HIGHBALL GLASS

**GARNISH:** GRAPEFRUIT WEDGE

1½ OZ. APEROL

1 OZ. SODA WATER

3 OZ. SPARKLING ROSÉ

Fill the highball glass with ice, add all of the ingredients, and gently stir.

Garnish with the grapefruit wedge and enjoy.

# ELEVATE

WITH ITS HINT OF SPARKLE, EVER-PRESENT EFFERVESCENCE, AND TYPICALLY SLEEK GLASSWARE, THE SPRITZ IS A DRINK THAT ADDS AN AIR OF SOPHISTICATION AND ELEGANCE TO ANY OCCASION.

# Violet Skies

*The rich blue hue here is a feast for the eyes, as is the layer of foam that sits atop the drink.*

**GLASSWARE:** COLLINS GLASS

**GARNISH:** NONE

- 2 OZ. GIN
- ¾ OZ. FRESH LEMON JUICE
- ½ OZ. CRÈME DE VIOLETTE
- ¼ OZ. ORGEAT
- ¼ OZ. RICH SIMPLE SYRUP (SEE PAGE 37)
- ½ OZ. EGG WHITE
- ¼ OZ. PASSION FRUIT SYRUP (SEE RECIPE)
- ¼ OZ. BLUE CURAÇAO
- 1 OZ. SPARKLING WATER, CHILLED, TO TOP

Place all of the ingredients, except for the sparkling water, in a cocktail shaker and dry shake for 10 seconds.

Add ice and shake vigorously until chilled.

Double strain over 2 ice cubes into the Collins glass, top with the sparkling water, and enjoy.

**PASSION FRUIT SYRUP:** Place 1½ cups passion fruit puree and 1½ cups Demerara Syrup (see page 16) in a mason jar, seal it, and shake until combined. Use immediately or store in the refrigerator.

# Paomo Ambrosia

*The cachaça and sake combined with yuzu juice and banana make this complex spritz effortless to consume.*

**GLASSWARE:** ROCKS GLASS

**GARNISH:** FINELY GROUND WHITE AMBROSIA TEA LEAVES

- 1½ OZ. CACHAÇA
- ½ OZ. SAKE
- 1 OZ. BANANA SYRUP (SEE RECIPE)
- ½ OZ. YUZU JUICE
- ¼ OZ. FRESH LEMON JUICE
- 2 CRUSHED SHISO LEAVES
- 1 EGG WHITE
- CLUB SODA, TO TOP

Place all of the ingredients, except for the club soda, in a cocktail shaker and dry shake for 10 seconds.

Add ice, shake until chilled, and double strain the cocktail over ice into the rocks glass.

Top with club soda, garnish with the ground tea leaves, and enjoy.

**BANANA SYRUP:** Place 5 peeled bananas and 4 cups Simple Syrup (see page 34) in a saucepan and bring to a boil. Cook for 5 minutes, reduce the heat to medium-low, and simmer for 15 minutes. Strain the syrup and let it cool completely before using or storing.

# Whistlepodu

*Rasam, a spicy-and-sour tomato soup popular in southern Indian cuisine, provides the inspiration for this ingenious cocktail, which is certain to elicit cheers from the entire crowd at your next brunch.*

**GLASSWARE:** ROCKS GLASS

**GARNISH:** FRIED CURRY LEAF

- 2 OZ. SMOKED RASAM (SEE RECIPE)
- 2 OZ. VODKA
- ¾ OZ. HONEY
- ¾ OZ. FRESH LIME JUICE
- 1 OZ. CLUB SODA

Place all of the ingredients in a mixing glass, stir to combine, and then carbonate the cocktail, using a SodaStream or similar appliance.

Pour the cocktail over ice into the rocks glass, garnish with the fried curry leaf, and enjoy.

**SMOKED RASAM:** Dice 15 tomatoes, place them in a saucepan, and cook over medium heat for about 20 minutes. Add coriander seeds, curry leaves, mustard seeds to taste, and the Masala Water (see recipe), stir to combine, and remove the pan from heat. Place the saucepan in a large roasting pan. Place hickory wood chips in a ramekin, coat a strip of paper towel with canola oil, and insert it in the center of the wood chips. Set the ramekin in the roasting pan, carefully light the wick, and wait until the wood chips ignite. Cover the roasting pan with aluminum foil and smoke the rasam for 1 hour.

**MASALA WATER:** Place 2 oz. dried mango in a bowl of hot water and soak it for 30 minutes. Place the rehydrated mango, 3 oz. cilantro, 3 green chile peppers, ½ teaspoon black pepper, ¼ teaspoon grated fresh ginger, and 2 teaspoons dried mint in a food processor and blitz until the mixture is a smooth paste. Stir the paste into 4 cups water and use as desired.

**SARSAPARILLA-INFUSED HONEY SYRUP:** Place 2 cups local honey, 1 cup hot water, and 1 oz. Indian sarsaparilla in a mason jar and stir to combine. Let the mixture steep for 24 hours. Strain before using or storing in the refrigerator.

**10 PERCENT SALINE SOLUTION:** Place 1 oz. salt in a measuring cup. Add warm water until you reach 10 oz. and the salt has dissolved. Let the solution cool before using or storing.

# The Beehive

*Don't be shy about experimenting with the saline solution used here in your other cocktail creations, as a little bit goes a long way.*

**GLASSWARE:** COLLINS GLASS

**GARNISH:** LEMON TWIST

- 1 OZ. SODA WATER
- 1½ OZ. THE BOTANIST ISLAY DRY GIN
- ¾ OZ. FRESH LEMON JUICE
- ¾ OZ. GINGER SOLUTION (SEE RECIPE)
- ½ OZ. SARSAPARILLA-INFUSED HONEY SYRUP (SEE RECIPE)
- 2 DASHES OF ORANGE BITTERS
- 2 DASHES OF 10 PERCENT SALINE SOLUTION (SEE RECIPE)

Pour the soda water into the Collins glass.

Place the remaining ingredients in a cocktail shaker, fill it two-thirds of the way with ice, and shake until chilled.

Strain the cocktail into the glass and add ice.

Garnish with the lemon twist and enjoy.

**GINGER SOLUTION:** Place ½ cup hot water, ½ cup evaporated cane sugar, and ½ cup freshly pressed ginger juice in a mason jar, stir until the sugar has dissolved, and enjoy.

# Crystal Gazpacho

*This cocktail provides a refreshing look into the culinary world's increasing influence on mixology.*

**GLASSWARE:** WINEGLASS

**GARNISH:** CUCUMBER SLICE, SPRIG OF FRESH ROSEMARY, 3 SLICES OF CHERRY TOMATO, 2 DASHES OF ORANGE-FLAVORED OLIVE OIL

- 1 OZ. TOMATO GIN (SEE RECIPE)
- 2 BAR SPOONS BREAD ST-GERMAIN (SEE RECIPE)
- 2 BAR SPOONS DRY VERMOUTH
- ½ OZ. TOMATO SHRUB (SEE RECIPE)
- 1⅓ OZ. TONIC WATER
- 1 OZ. SODA WATER

Place gin, St-Germain, vermouth, and shrub in a cocktail shaker and dry shake for 15 seconds.

Pour over ice into the wineglass and top with the tonic water and soda water.

Garnish with the cucumber slice, fresh rosemary, slices of cherry tomato, and olive oil and enjoy.

**TOMATO GIN:** Place 6 cherry tomatoes and 1 cup Beefeater 24 gin in a blender and puree until smooth. Pour the mixture into a mason jar and chill in the refrigerator for 3 hours. Strain through a coffee filter before using or storing.

**BREAD ST-GERMAIN:** Place 1 oz. of French bread and 7 oz. St-Germain in a vacuum bag, vacuum seal it, and sous vide at 140°F for 2 hours. Remove the vacuum bag from the water bath and let the mixture cool completely. Strain through a coffee filter before using or storing.

**TOMATO SHRUB:** Place 5 tomatoes in a blender and puree until smooth. Strain the puree through a coffee filter until you have 10 oz. of tomato water, leaving the puree overnight if necessary. Place the tomato water and 5 oz. sugar in a saucepan and bring it to a simmer over low heat, stirring to dissolve the sugar. Cook for 5 minutes, stir in a splash of white balsamic vinegar, and let the shrub cool completely before using or storing.

# Beyond the Sea

*Any gin will work here, but the suggested offering from Oakland Spirits Company will make a noticeable difference, as it is packed with notes of foraged nori, lemongrass, and some other elements of California's coastal terroir.*

**GLASSWARE:** COLLINS GLASS

**GARNISH:** 2 SHEETS OF NORI, SHREDDED

- 2 OZ. OAKLAND SPIRITS CO. AUTOMATIC SEA GIN
- ¾ OZ. SEAWEED-INFUSED HONEY (SEE RECIPE)
- ½ OZ. FRESH LEMON JUICE
- ½ OZ. FRESH LIME JUICE
- 4 DASHES OF CHAMOMILE TINCTURE
- SODA WATER, TO TOP

Place all of the ingredients, except for the soda water, in a cocktail shaker, fill it two-thirds of the way with ice, and shake until chilled.

Double strain into the Collins glass, top with soda water, and gently stir.

Garnish with the shredded nori and enjoy.

**SEAWEED-INFUSED HONEY:** Place ½ cup honey and ½ cup boiling water in a mason jar and stir until well combined. Add 1 sheet of dried nori and let the mixture sit at room temperature. Strain before using or storing, making sure to press down on the nori to extract as much liquid and flavor as possible.

# Cool as Moons

*A refreshing, sweet, and sour drink that will hit the spot when you want dessert, but don't have room for something heavy.*

**GLASSWARE:** HIGHBALL GLASS

**GARNISH:** DEHYDRATED LIME WHEEL, FRESH MINT, MARASCHINO CHERRY

- 1⅜ oz. Kaffir Lime Leaf–Infused Gin (see recipe)
- ½ oz. Pear Brandy
- ½ oz. Giffard Rhubarb Liqueur
- 1 oz. Cranberry Juice
- ¾ oz. Fresh Lemon Juice
- Sparkling Wine, to top

Place all of the ingredients, except for the sparkling wine, in a cocktail shaker, fill it two-thirds of the way with ice, and shake until chilled.

Strain over ice into the highball glass and top with sparkling wine.

Garnish with the dehydrated lime wheel, fresh mint, and maraschino cherry and enjoy.

**KAFFIR LIME LEAF–INFUSED GIN:** Place 10 to 12 kaffir lime leaves and a 750 ml bottle of gin in a large mason jar and stir vigorously for 1 minute. Steep for 12 hours and strain before using or storing.

**GINGER SYRUP:** Place 1 cup water and 1 cup sugar in a saucepan and bring the mixture to a boil, stirring to dissolve the sugar. Add a peeled 1-inch piece of fresh ginger, remove the pan from heat, and let the syrup cool completely. Strain before using or storing.

# Cauldron Cure

*The taste is not far behind, but the best feature of this potion is that the color will start changing after you've taken the first few sips.*

**GLASSWARE:** SNIFTER

**GARNISH:** 1 TEASPOON BUTTERFLY PEA FLOWER EXTRACT

- 1½ OZ. TRIPLE CITRUS–INFUSED GIN (SEE RECIPE)
- ⅞ OZ. FRESH LEMON JUICE
- ⅞ OZ. BOTTLEGREEN RHUBARB & GINGER CORDIAL
- 1 TEASPOON GINGER SYRUP (SEE RECIPE)
- 1 OZ. CHAMPAGNE

Place all of the ingredients, except for the Champagne, in a cocktail shaker, fill it two-thirds of the way with ice, and shake until chilled.

Double strain over ice into the chosen glass and top with the Champagne.

Garnish with the butterfly pea flower extract, letting it filter down through the cocktail.

**TRIPLE CITRUS–INFUSED GIN:** Place the whole peels of a lemon, an orange, and a grapefruit and a 750 ml bottle of London dry gin in a mason jar and steep for 24 hours. Strain before using or storing.

# La Diosa

*The Pineapple Marmalade is far more complex than it seems on its face, and as such is an ingredient you will be continually searching for other places to incorporate it.*

**GLASSWARE:** COUPE

**GARNISH:** EDIBLE FLOWER BLOSSOMS, HOUSE TAJÍN (SEE RECIPE)

- 1½ OZ. TEQUILA
- ¾ OZ. TRIPLE SEC
- ½ OZ. FRESH LIME JUICE
- 1 TABLESPOON PINEAPPLE MARMALADE (SEE RECIPE)
- ½ TEASPOON RED PEPPER FLAKES
- 1 SMALL BUNCH OF FRESH CILANTRO
- 1 OZ. SODA WATER, TO TOP

Place all of the ingredients, except for the soda water, in a cocktail shaker, fill it two-thirds of the way with ice, and shake until chilled.

Strain the cocktail, remove the ice from the shaker, and place the cocktail back in the shaker. Add the soda water and shake for 10 seconds.

Strain the cocktail into the coupe, garnish with the edible flower blossoms and House Tajín, and enjoy.

**PINEAPPLE MARMALADE:** Place the chopped flesh of 4 pineapples, 8 cinnamon sticks, ¼ cup pure vanilla extract, 4 orange peels, 2 deseeded dried guajillo chile peppers, 1 cup sweet vermouth, 1 cup Lillet Blanc, and 4 cups sugar in a saucepan and simmer gently the until the liquid has reduced by at least half, 4 to 5 hours. Remove the cinnamon sticks and chiles, place the marmalade in a blender, and puree until smooth. Let the marmalade cool before using or storing.

**HOUSE TAJÍN:** Place 1 cup mesquite seasoning, 1 cup smoked paprika, ½ cup kosher salt, and the zest of 2 grapefruits in a container and stir to combine. Use as desired.

**FIG CORDIAL:** Preheat the oven to 350°F. Place 15 quartered figs on a parchment-lined baking sheet, drizzle 3½ oz. honey over them, and then sprinkle 1¾ oz. walnuts around the pan. Place the pan in the oven and bake for 10 minutes. While the figs and walnuts are in the oven, place the Fig Leaf Syrup (see recipe) in a saucepan and warm it over medium heat. When the figs and walnuts are done, remove them from the oven, add them to the syrup, and simmer for 10 minutes. Strain the mixture into a mason jar, stir in 1 tablespoon citric acid and 7 oz. rosé, and let the cordial cool completely before using or storing.

**FIG LEAF SYRUP:** Place 30 fig leaves in a container and pour 3 cups of warm Simple Syrup (see page 34) over them. Steep for 30 minutes and strain before using or storing.

# Diablo Otoño

*A light but surprisingly complex drink, thanks to the inventive Fig Cordial and the slightly bitter note added by the tonic water.*

**GLASSWARE:** COLLINS GLASS

**GARNISH:** NONE

- 1 OZ. TEQUILA
- 1 OZ. FIG CORDIAL (SEE RECIPE)
- 1 TEASPOON FIG LIQUEUR
- TONIC WATER, TO TOP

Place three ice spheres in the Collins glass. Add all of the ingredients, except for the tonic water, and stir until chilled.

Top with tonic water and enjoy.

# Cucumber Collins

*Along with the Chartreuse Swizzle, this is one of the Bay Area's signature twenty-first century drinks.*

**GLASSWARE:** COLLINS GLASS

**GARNISH:** ENGLISH CUCUMBER SLICES, PICKLED PURPLE CUCUMBERS (SEE RECIPE), PICKLED HUCKLEBERRIES (SEE RECIPE)

- 1½ OZ. SQUARE ONE CUCUMBER VODKA
- ½ OZ. FRESH LEMON JUICE
- ¼ OZ. FRESH YUZU JUICE
- ½ OZ. SIMPLE SYRUP (SEE PAGE 34)
- 1½ OZ. SODA WATER

Place the vodka, juices, and syrup in the short half of a Boston shaker. Fill it to the top with ice and seal it.

Shake just a few times to mix the cocktail. Unseal the shaker, leaving everything in the larger half.

Add the soda water to the mixture and swirl it around a few times to incorporate.

Pour the contents of the shaker into the Collins glass, garnish with the cucumbers and huckleberries, and enjoy.

**PICKLED PURPLE CUCUMBERS:** Place 3 cups Pickled Huckleberry brine and 3 cups thinly sliced English cucumbers in a large container, cover it, and refrigerate for 24 hours before using.

**PICKLED HUCKLEBERRIES:** Place 6 cups unseasoned rice vinegar, 2 cups mirin, and 2 cups sake in a large saucepan and bring to a boil. Add 3 cups sugar and stir to dissolve. Add 2 lbs. wild huckleberries and bring to a boil. Remove the pan from heat and let the mixture cool. Strain, making sure to reserve 3 cups of brine for the Pickled Purple Cucumbers, before using or storing.

# Seville Spritz

*If you are a fan of orange, you've found your drink. And if you're not, you will be soon enough.*

**GLASSWARE:** HIGHBALL GLASS

**GARNISH:** BLOOD ORANGE WHEEL, ORANGE TWIST

| | |
|---|---|
| 1 | OZ. TANQUERAY SEVILLA ORANGE |
| 1 | OZ. ORANGE WINE |
| ½ | OZ. VANILLA SYRUP (SEE PAGE 138) |
| 2 | DASHES OF ORANGE BITTERS |
| ½ | OZ. PIERRE FERRAND DRY CURAÇAO |
| | DROP OF ORANGE BLOSSOM WATER |
| 3 | OZ. PROSECCO |

Place all of the ingredients, except for the prosecco, in a cocktail shaker, fill it two-thirds of the way with ice, and shake until chilled.

Strain over ice into the highball glass, top with the prosecco, and gently stir.

Garnish with the blood orange wheel and orange twist and enjoy.

# Milk Beach

*The almond milk may seem odd in a spritz, but it not only makes the drink prettier, it smooths it out as well.*

**GLASSWARE:** COLLINS GLASS
**GARNISH:** STRIP OF LEMON PEEL

| | |
|---|---|
| | GROUND PISTACHIOS, FOR THE RIM |
| | SALT, FOR THE RIM |
| 2 | OZ. ALMOND MILK |
| 1⅔ | OZ. ITALICUS ROSOLIO DI BERGAMOTTO |
| ½ | OZ. FRESH LEMON JUICE |
| ⅙ | OZ. SIMPLE SYRUP (SEE PAGE 34) |
| 1⅔ | OZ. LEMON SODA |

Combine the pistachios and salt in a small dish. Wet the rim of the Collins glass and rim it with the mixture. Add one or two ice cubes to the glass.

Place the almond milk, Italicus, lemon juice, and syrup in a cocktail shaker, fill it two-thirds of the way with ice, and shake until chilled.

Strain into the Collins glass and top with the soda.

Garnish with the strip of lemon peel and enjoy.

# No One Mourns the Wicked

*Try not to overdo it with the soda water—you want just enough to open up the bold ingredients here.*

**GLASSWARE:** WINEGLASS

**GARNISH:** BLACK LICORICE RIBBON

- ½ OZ. COINTREAU
- ½ OZ. CHAMBORD
- ½ OZ. RASPBERRY BALSAMIC VINEGAR
- ⅚ OZ. GALLIANO SAMBUCA BLACK
- SODA WATER, TO TOP

Place all of the ingredients, except for the soda water, in a cocktail shaker, fill it two-thirds of the way with ice, and shake until chilled.

Strain over ice into the wineglass and top with soda water.

Garnish with the black licorice ribbon and enjoy.

# Balearica

*More than perhaps any other drink in the book, this one is best enjoyed with a sunset.*

**GLASSWARE:** GOBLET

**GARNISH:** CARDAMOM SEEDS, FRESH BASIL, GRAPEFRUIT SLICE

| | |
|---|---|
| 2 | OZ. GRAPEFRUIT JUICE |
| 1 | OZ. TANQUERAY NO. TEN |
| 1 | OZ. APEROL |
| ½ | OZ. FRESH LIME JUICE |
| ⅓ | OZ. GRENADINE |
| 1 | TEASPOON CARDAMOM SEEDS |
| 3 | FRESH BASIL LEAVES |
| 2 | OZ. SPARKLING WATER |

Place all of the ingredients, except for the sparkling water, in a cocktail shaker, fill it two-thirds of the way with ice, and shake until chilled.

Double strain over ice into the goblet and top with sparkling water.

Garnish with additional cardamom and fresh basil and the grapefruit slice and enjoy.

# Bocanada

*Translated as "breath of fresh air," this drink is, as you would expect, refreshing and easy to sip. But it is also rich, complex, and carries a generous kick.*

**GLASSWARE:** ROCKS GLASS

**GARNISH:** LIME WEDGE, KALE

- 1½ OZ. GREEN RAICILLA (SEE RECIPE)
- ¾ OZ. FINO SHERRY
- TONIC WATER, TO TOP

Place all of the ingredients, except for the tonic water, in a mixing glass, fill it two-thirds of the way with ice, and stir until chilled.

Strain over ice into the rocks glass and top with tonic water.

Garnish with the lime wedge and kale and enjoy.

**GREEN RAICILLA:** Place ⅓ oz. scarlet kale, 2½ oz. avocado leaves, 6¾ oz. avocado oil, and a 750 ml bottle of Raicilla in a vacuum bag and sous vide at 158°F for 2 hours. Remove the bag from the water bath and refrigerate it overnight. Strain before using or storing.

# Saffron Spritz

*This balanced, low-ABV serve is a perfect aperitif. It's also a worthy use of one of the world's most expensive substances—saffron.*

**GLASSWARE:** CHAMPAGNE FLUTE

**GARNISH:** EDIBLE FLOWER PETAL

- 1 ⅔ OZ. APPLE-INFUSED ROSÉ (SEE RECIPE)
- ⅔ OZ. FRESH LEMON JUICE
- ¾ OZ. SAFFRON HONEY (SEE RECIPE)
- FEVER-TREE MEDITERRANEAN TONIC WATER, TO TOP

Place all of the ingredients, except for the tonic water, in a mixing glass, fill it two-thirds of the way with ice, and stir until chilled.

Strain into the Champagne flute and top with tonic water.

Garnish with the edible flower petal and enjoy.

**APPLE-INFUSED ROSÉ:** Place 6 apple peels and 13½ oz. dry rosé in a mason jar, seal it, and shake. Let the mixture steep in the refrigerator for 3 days. Strain before using or storing.

**SAFFRON HONEY:** Place 1 cup honey and ½ cup hot water in a mason jar and stir to combine. While stirring, gradually add ¼ teaspoon saffron threads. Let the mixture steep for 2 days. Strain before using or storing.

**MELON JUICE:** Place 2 cups chopped cantaloupe and ¾ cup water in a blender and puree on high until smooth. Strain before using or storing.

# Sitting in Trees

*The creamy, subtle flavor of cantaloupe and the anise-edged infused tequila pair to provide the backbone of this particularly bracing cocktail.*

**GLASSWARE:** HIGHBALL GLASS

**GARNISH:** HONEYDEW MELON SLICE

- 1⅙ OZ. DRY ROSÉ WINE
- ⅔ OZ. FENNEL-INFUSED TEQUILA (SEE RECIPE)
- 1 BAR SPOON FRESH LEMON JUICE
- ⅓ OZ. MELON JUICE (SEE RECIPE)
- ⅖ OZ. VANILLA SYRUP (SEE PAGE 138)
-   SODA WATER, TO TOP

Place all of the ingredients, except for the soda water, in a cocktail shaker, fill it two-thirds of the way with ice, and shake until chilled.

Strain over ice into the highball glass and top with soda water.

Garnish with the honeydew melon slice and enjoy.

**FENNEL-INFUSED TEQUILA:** Lightly crush 1½ teaspoons fennel seeds and place them in a mason jar. Add 10 oz. tequila and steep for 2 hours. Strain before using or storing.

# CELEBRATE

AS EVERYONE KNOWS, WHEN THE TIME COMES TO TRULY REJOICE, BUBBLES HAVE TO BE PRESENT. THIS POSITIONS THE SPRITZ AS THE VERY BEST COCKTAIL OPTION FOR A PARTY, AND ITS LIGHT, LOW-ABV CHARACTER MEANS THAT YOU CAN INDULGE WITHOUT WORRYING ABOUT PAYING THE PRICE FOR IT LATER.

# French 75

*For the gin component, try swapping in Old Tom gin, as its sweetness relative to London dry–styled gins could be a brilliant fit here.*

**GLASSWARE:** CHAMPAGNE FLUTE

**GARNISH:** LEMON TWIST, MARASCHINO CHERRY

| | |
|---|---|
| 1 | SUGAR CUBE |
| | JUICE OF 1 LEMON WEDGE |
| 1 | OZ. GIN |
| 2 | OZ. CHAMPAGNE |

Place the sugar cube in the Champagne flute and add the lemon juice.

Add the gin and top with the Champagne.

Garnish the cocktail with the lemon twist. Skewer the cherry with a toothpick and place it over the mouth of the champagne flute.

# Martínez Spritz

*Authentic, relaxed, and friendly—that's the atmosphere where this cocktail was crafted in the heart of Mexico City. The result of this recipe is a tropical and sparkling mix.*

**GLASSWARE:** WINEGLASS

**GARNISH:** BEE POLLEN

- 1½ OZ. WHITE WINE
- 1 OZ. PASSION FRUIT JUICE
- 1 OZ. CINZANO ROSSO VERMOUTH
- ½ OZ. SIMPLE SYRUP (SEE PAGE 34)
- SPARKLING WINE, TO TOP

Fill the wineglass with ice, add the white wine, juice, vermouth, and syrup, and stir until chilled.

Top with sparkling wine, garnish with bee pollen, and enjoy.

# Ritz Spritz

*The Ritz Spritz manages to be both elegant and playful at once, taking classic flavor combinations and punching them up with a bit of fizz. It's sweet, citrusy, and absolutely delicious.*

**GLASSWARE:** COUPE

**GARNISH:** ORANGE TWIST

- ¾ OZ. COGNAC
- ½ OZ. CURAÇAO
- ¼ OZ. LUXARDO MARASCHINO LIQUEUR
- ¼ OZ. FRESH LEMON JUICE
- CHAMPAGNE, CHILLED, TO TOP

Chill the coupe in the freezer.

Place the Cognac, curaçao, and Luxardo in a mixing glass, fill it two-thirds of the way with ice, and stir until chilled.

Strain into the chilled coupe and top with Champagne.

Garnish with the orange twist and enjoy.

# Brighter Days

*If the thought of egg white in a cocktail makes you a little anxious, feel free to forgo it here.*

 **GLASSWARE:** CHAMPAGNE FLUTE

**GARNISH:** NONE

| | |
|---|---|
| 1½ | OZ. EFFEN BLOOD ORANGE VODKA |
| ¾ | OZ. APEROL |
| 1 | OZ. FRESH LEMON JUICE |
| ½ | OZ. SIMPLE SYRUP (SEE PAGE 34) |
| ½ | OZ. EGG WHITE |
| 1 | OZ. PROSECCO, PLUS MORE TO TOP |

Chill the Champagne flute in the freezer.

Place all of the ingredients, except for the prosecco, in a cocktail shaker containing 1 large ice cube and shake until chilled.

Pour the prosecco into the chilled Champagne flute and strain the cocktail over it.

Top with additional prosecco and enjoy.

# California Cooler

*If you're looking for direction regarding the cordial, choose a Sauvignon Blanc that is dry with tropical and muscat notes.*

**GLASSWARE:** COUPE

**GARNISH:** FRESH THYME

- 1½ OZ. GIN
- ¾ OZ. FRESHLY PRESSED CELERY JUICE
- ½ OZ. SAUVIGNON BLANC & THYME CORDIAL (SEE RECIPE)
- ½ OZ. FRESH LIME JUICE
- 1 OZ. CHAMPAGNE

Place all of the ingredients, except for the Champagne, in a cocktail shaker, fill it two-thirds of the way with ice, and shake until chilled.

Double strain into the coupe and top with the Champagne.

Garnish with fresh thyme and enjoy.

### SAUVIGNON BLANC & THYME CORDIAL:
Place 750 ml Sauvignon Blanc in a saucepan and bring to a gentle boil. Reduce the heat and simmer the wine for 10 minutes. Add ½ bunch of fresh thyme and a small chunk of fresh horseradish, peeled and lightly crushed, reduce the heat to low, and cook for 10 minutes. Add 4 cups sugar and stir until it has dissolved. Remove the pan from heat and let it cool completely. Strain before using or storing.

# 47 Monkeys

*Sloe berries, the fruit of the blackthorn shrub, are macerated in gin to provide the crimson color and warm, fruity taste sloe gin is known for.*

**GLASSWARE:** WINEGLASS

**GARNISH:** 2 SLICED STRAWBERRIES, FRESH BASIL

| | |
|---|---|
| 3 | STRAWBERRIES |
| 2 | TO 3 FRESH BASIL LEAVES |
| ⅞ | OZ. MONKEY 47 SCHWARZWALD SLOE GIN |
| ⅞ | OZ. MONKEY 47 SCHWARZWALD DRY GIN |
| ¾ | OZ. FRESH LIME JUICE |
| 2 | DASHES OF PEYCHAUD'S BITTERS |
| | CHAMPAGNE, TO TOP |

Place the strawberries in a cocktail shaker and muddle.

Slap the basil leaves and add them to the shaker along with ice, the gins, lime juice, and bitters. Shake until chilled.

Double strain over ice into the wineglass.

Top with the Champagne, garnish with the sliced strawberries and fresh basil, and enjoy.

# Port in a Storm

*The bit of spice from the Cinnamon Syrup really stands out in this light and tart cocktail.*

**GLASSWARE:** CHAMPAGNE FLUTE

**GARNISH:** GRAPEFRUIT TWIST

- ¾ OZ. TEQUILA
- 1¼ OZ. RUBY RED GRAPEFRUIT JUICE
- 1¼ OZ. WHITE GRAPEFRUIT JUICE
- DASH OF CINNAMON SYRUP (SEE RECIPE)
- CHAMPAGNE, TO TOP

Place all of the ingredients, except for the Champagne, in the champagne flute and stir to combine.

Top with Champagne, garnish with the grapefruit twist, and enjoy.

**CINNAMON SYRUP:** Place 1 cup water and 2 cinnamon sticks in a saucepan and bring the mixture to a boil. Add 2 cups sugar and stir until it has dissolved. Remove the pan from heat, cover it, and let the mixture steep at room temperature for 12 hours. Strain the syrup through cheesecloth before using or storing.

**JASMINE-INFUSED VODKA:** Place a 750 ml bottle of vodka and 3 tablespoons of loose-leaf jasmine tea in a mason jar and steep for 3 to 4 hours. Strain before using or storing.

**LIME & SAGE CORDIAL:** Place 11 oz. fresh lime juice and 21 oz. caster (superfine) sugar in a saucepan and bring to a simmer, stirring to dissolve the sugar. Stir in 1½ oz. chopped lime peel and 1½ oz. fresh sage leaves, cook for 5 minutes, and remove the pan from heat. When the mixture has cooled, pour it into a mason jar, cover, and let the mixture steep for 4 hours. Strain the cordial before using or storing in the refrigerator.

# Pride

*The Pride is inspired by Oscar Wilde's two favorite drinks, absinthe and Champagne, with the former's aroma being articulated by the combination of Jasmine-Infused Vodka and the star anise extract.*

**GLASSWARE:** COUPE

**GARNISH:** STRIP FASHIONED FROM 1 PAGE OF *THE PICTURE OF DORIAN GRAY*

| | |
|---|---|
| 1 | **OZ. JASMINE-INFUSED VODKA (SEE RECIPE)** |
| 1 | **OZ. LIME & SAGE CORDIAL (SEE RECIPE)** |
| | **CHAMPAGNE, TO TOP** |
| | **STAR ANISE EXTRACT, TO MIST** |

Place the vodka and cordial in a cocktail shaker, fill it two-thirds of the way with ice, and shake until chilled.

Strain into the coupe and top with Champagne.

Place the star anise extract in an atomizer and mist the cocktail with it.

Tie the paper strip to the stem of the glass and enjoy.

# Trench 75

*Nikka Coffey gin is more citrusy than juniper-forward, which means it plays well with others. Here, it provides an opportunity for the sparkling sake to shine.*

**GLASSWARE:** COUPE

**GARNISH:** DEHYDRATED LIME WHEEL

- 1 OZ. NIKKA COFFEY GIN
- ½ OZ. FRESH LEMON JUICE
- 2 BAR SPOONS HONEY WATER (SEE PAGE 33)
- 1 OZ. SPARKLING SAKE

Place the gin, lemon juice, and Honey Water in a cocktail shaker, fill it two-thirds of the way with ice, and shake until chilled.

Strain into the coupe and top with the sparkling sake.

Garnish with the dehydrated lime wheel and enjoy.

# The Jerome

*Verjus, the juice of unripe wine grapes, is becoming an increasingly common cocktail component, as it is capable of adding a sour element without also introducing acid to the equation.*

**GLASSWARE:** COUPE

**GARNISH:** STRIP OF LEMON PEEL

- 1½ OZ. CALVADOS VSOP
- 1 TEASPOON SUZE
- ½ OZ. PIERRE FERRAND COGNAC
- ⅞ OZ. VERJUS
- 2 DASHES OF ORANGE BITTERS
- 2 TEASPOONS RICH SIMPLE SYRUP (SEE PAGE 37)
- 2 DASHES OF PEYCHAUD'S BITTERS
- 1¾ OZ. CHAMPAGNE

Place all of the ingredients, except for the Champagne, in a mixing glass, add a large ice cube, and stir until chilled.

Strain into the coupe and top with the Champagne.

Garnish with the strip of lemon peel and enjoy.

# Tropical Bird Spritz

*A really fun way to start off an evening. The vermouth is nice and bitter, the elderflower liqueur is sweet, the pineapple is tart and fruity, and the prosecco and soda water provide the bubbles. What more could you ask for?*

**GLASSWARE:** COLLINS GLASS

**GARNISH:** LIME WHEELS

- 1½ OZ. MARTINI & ROSSI RISERVA SPECIALE BITTER VERMOUTH
- 1 OZ. MARTINI & ROSSI PROSECCO
- 1 OZ. SODA WATER
- ½ OZ. ST-GERMAIN
- ½ OZ. PINEAPPLE SHRUB (SEE RECIPE)

Fill the Collins glass with ice, add all of the ingredients, and stir until chilled.

Garnish with the lime wheels and enjoy.

**PINEAPPLE SHRUB:** Place ½ cup Champagne vinegar, ½ cup sugar, and ¼ cup chopped pineapple in a saucepan and bring to a boil, stirring to dissolve the sugar. Cook for 5 minutes, remove the pan from heat, and let the shrub cool completely. Strain before using or storing.

# Orphic Flowers

*Looking to class up cocktail hour? The stunning, amber-hued Orphic Flowers is tough to improve upon.*

**GLASSWARE:** CHAMPAGNE COUPE

**GARNISH:** DROP OF SPRUCE EXTRACT, EDIBLE FLOWER BLOSSOMS

| | |
|---|---|
| 1 | SUGAR CUBE |
| 2 | DASHES OF ANGOSTURA BITTERS |
| 1⅔ | OZ. BRANDY |
| | CHAMPAGNE, TO TOP |

Place the sugar cube in the Champagne coupe and moisten it with the bitters.

Place the brandy in a mixing glass, fill it two-thirds of the way with ice, and stir until chilled.

Strain over the ice cube and top with Champagne.

Garnish with the spruce extract and edible flower blossoms and enjoy.

# Mystic Beauty

*A little secret: by adding a bit of bright acidity, you can elevate a humble sparkling wine to the lofty heights typically reserved for Champagne. Here, that acidity comes in the form of lemon juice and the shrub.*

**GLASSWARE:** COUPE

**GARNISH:** STRIP OF LEMON PEEL

- 1⅔ **OZ. LONDON DRY GIN**
- ⅘ **OZ. FRESH LEMON JUICE**
- ⅓ **OZ. EGG WHITE**
- ⅔ **OZ. RASPBERRY SHRUB (SEE RECIPE)**
- **PROSECCO, TO TOP**

Place all of the ingredients, except for the prosecco, in a cocktail shaker, fill it two-thirds of the way with ice, and shake until chilled.

Strain into the coupe and top with prosecco.

Garnish with the strip of lemon peel and enjoy.

**RASPBERRY SHRUB:** Place 500 grams raspberries and 800 grams caster (superfine) sugar in a large mason jar and mash until the sugar is dissolved. Let the mixture macerate for 24 hours. Add 400 grams apple cider vinegar and shake until combined. Strain the shrub before using or storing.

# Cometa

*The guava juice lends the irresistible hue, and the fino sherry and Yellow Chartreuse supply a depth that will linger long past when you are finished with this one.*

**GLASSWARE:** ROCKS GLASS

**GARNISH:** BANANA LEAVES, EDIBLE PINK ROSE

- 1½ OZ. MEZCAL
- 1½ OZ. GUAVA JUICE
- ½ OZ. YELLOW CHARTREUSE
- ½ OZ. FINO SHERRY
- ½ OZ. AGAVE NECTAR
- ½ OZ. FRESH LEMON JUICE
- SODA WATER, TO TOP

Place all of the ingredients, except for the soda water, in a cocktail shaker, fill it two-thirds of the way with ice, and shake until chilled.

Strain over ice into the rocks glass and top with soda.

Garnish with the banana leaves and rose and enjoy.

# Hidden Sweet

*Champagne rosé works really well with brown sugar and cognac. The sugar cube will dissolve, giving Hidden Sweet more sweetness. So sip it slowly.*

**GLASSWARE:** CHAMPAGNE FLUTE
**GARNISH:** NONE

| | |
|---|---|
| 1 | **BROWN SUGAR CUBE** |
| | **DASH OF ANGOSTURA BITTERS** |
| ¾ | **OZ. COGNAC** |
| 3 | **OZ. ROSÉ CHAMPAGNE** |

Chill the Champagne flute in the freezer.

Place the sugar cube in the glass and moisten it with the bitters.

Add the Cognac and rosé Champagne and enjoy.

# CONVERSION TABLE

## WEIGHTS

1 oz. = 28 grams
2 oz. = 57 grams
4 oz. (¼ lb.) = 113 grams
8 oz. (½ lb.) = 227 grams
16 oz. (1 lb.) = 454 grams

## VOLUME MEASURES

⅛ teaspoon = 0.6 ml
¼ teaspoon = 1.23 ml
½ teaspoon = 2.5 ml
1 teaspoon = 5 ml
1 tablespoon (3 teaspoons) = ½ fluid oz. = 15 ml
2 tablespoons = 1 fluid oz. = 29.5 ml
¼ cup (4 tablespoons) = 2 fluid oz. = 59 ml
⅓ cup (5⅓ tablespoons) = 2.7 fluid oz. = 80 ml
½ cup (8 tablespoons) = 4 fluid oz. = 120 ml
⅔ cup (10⅔ tablespoons) = 5.4 fluid oz. = 160 ml
¾ cup (12 tablespoons) = 6 fluid oz. = 180 ml
1 cup (16 tablespoons) = 8 fluid oz. = 240 ml

## TEMPERATURE EQUIVALENTS

| °F | °C | Gas Mark |
|---|---|---|
| 225 | 110 | ¼ |
| 250 | 130 | ½ |
| 275 | 140 | 1 |
| 300 | 150 | 2 |
| 325 | 170 | 3 |
| 350 | 180 | 4 |
| 375 | 190 | 5 |
| 400 | 200 | 6 |
| 425 | 220 | 7 |
| 450 | 230 | 8 |
| 475 | 240 | 9 |
| 500 | 250 | 10 |

## LENGTH MEASURES

1/16 inch = 1.6 mm
⅛ inch = 3 mm
¼ inch = 6.35 mm
½ inch = 1.25 cm
¾ inch = 2 cm
1 inch = 2.5 cm

# INDEX

**A**

absinthe, Extra Sonic, 54
Acqua Di Cedro Nardini, High C Spritz, 77
agave nectar
   Cometa, 212
   Piscomelo, 142
   Sage & Mint Agave, 24
Alizé Gold Passion, Purple Rain, 93
Amaro Nonino, Ananda Spritz, 17
Americano recipe, 38
Ananda Spritz recipe, 17
Angostura bitters
   Ananda Spritz, 17
   Apple of Your Eye, 18
   Aroma, 122
   Diciotto, 53
   Hidden Sweet, 213
   Orphic Flowers, 209
Aperol
   Aperol Spritz, 10
   Balearica, 178
   Brighter Days, 193
   Go Ahead, Romeo, 13
   Pink Sky, 72
   Sunlit Horizon, 149
Aperol Ice Cubes recipe, 13
Aperol Spritz recipe, 10
apple cider vinegar
   Strawberry Vinegar, 76
   Watermelon Shrub, 90
Apple-Infused Rosé, Saffron Spritz, 182
Apple-Infused Rosé recipe, 182
Apple of Your Eye recipe, 18
apples/apple juice
   Apple-Infused Rosé, 182
   Apple of Your Eye, 18
   Apple Syrup, 19
Apple Syrup recipe, 19
Appleton Estate Signature Blend Rum, El Cuco, 81
apricot liqueur, Mind Games, 141
aquavit, Farm & Vine, 29
Aroma recipe, 122

**B**

Bacardí Rum, Fruits of the Monastic Life, 117
Balearica recipe, 178
bananas
   Banana Syrup, 153
   Cometa, 212
Banana Syrup recipe, 153
basil
   47 Monkeys, 197
   Balearica, 178
   Basilico, 75
   Basil Syrup, 100
   Floating Leaf, 101
   Rosa Spritz, 62
Basilico recipe, 75
Basil Syrup recipe, 100
Beefeater 24 Gin, Tomato Gin, 158
The Beehive recipe, 157
beets/beet juice, The Garden, 71
Bellini recipe, 110
Beluga Noble Vodka, Pacific Rhythms, 66
berries. *See also* strawberry
   Cherry Valance, 119
   Sacred Lotus, 26
Berries & Bubbles recipe, 113
Beverly Interpretation recipe, 126
Beyond the Sea recipe, 161
blended Scotch whisky, Kissed By a Rose, 134
blood oranges/blood orange juice
   Mind Games, 141
   Seville Spritz, 173
Blue Curaçao, Violet Skies, 152
Bocanada recipe, 181
Bordiga Maraschino Liqueur, Sour Cherry Spritz, 61
Botanical Garden Spritz recipe, 21
Bottlegreen Elderflower Cordial, Rose Blossom, 30
Bottlegreen Rhubarb & Ginger Cordial, Cauldron Cure, 165
brandy, Orphic Flowers, 209
brandy snifter, Go Ahead, Romeo, 13
Bread St-Germain recipe, 159
Brighter Days recipe, 193
Broken Bicyclette recipe, 58
butterfly pea flower extract, 165

**C**

cachaça, Paomo Ambrosia, 153
California Cooler recipe, 194
Calvados, Deci's Roommate, 37
Calvados VSOP, The Jerome, 205
Campari
   Americano, 38
   Campari Seltz, 49
   Lady in Red, 76
   Mi-Và, 129
   Negroni Sbagliato, 42
   Running Up That Hill, 133
Campari Seltz recipe, 49
Caña Brava 7 Year Rum, El Cuco, 81
caster (superfine) sugar
   Fruits of the Monastic Life, 117
   Lime & Sage Cordial, 200

Raspberry Cordial, 92
Raspberry Shrub, 210
Rossini, 120
Cauldron Cure recipe, 165
Celebrate
   47 Monkeys, 197
   Brighter Days, 193
   California Cooler, 194
   Cometa, 212
   French 75, 188
   Hidden Sweet, 213
   The Jerome, 205
   Martínez Spritz, 189
   Mystic Beauty, 210
   Orphic Flowers, 209
   Port in a Storm, 198
   Pride, 201
   Ritz Spritz, 190
   Trench 75, 202
   Tropical Bird Spritz, 206
Champagne
   Bellini, 110
   Berries & Bubbles, 113
   California Cooler, 194
   Cauldron Cure, 165
   Diciotto, 53
   French 75, 188
   I Wish I Was in New Orleans, 78
   The Jerome, 205
   Mimosa, 109
   Orphic Flowers, 209
   Port in a Storm, 198
   Pride, 201
   Ritz Spritz, 190
Champagne coupe, Orphic Flowers, 209
Champagne flute
   Basilico, 75
   Bellini, 110
   Beverly Interpretation, 126
   Brighter Days, 193

Formosa Fizz, 69
French 75, 188
Hidden Sweet, 213
High C Spritz, 77
I Wish I Was in New Orleans, 78
Mimosa, 109
Port in a Storm, 198
Rossini, 120
Saffron Spritz, 182
Stranger Things, 82
Veruschka, 125
Cherry Valance recipe, 119
cilantro
   La Diosa, 166
   Masala Water, 155
cinnamon
   Cinnamon Syrup, 198
   Pineapple Marmalade, 166
Cinnamon Syrup recipe, 198
Cinzano 1757 Vermouth Di Torino Gi Rosso
   Americano, 38
   Negroni Shagliato, 42
Cinzano Prosecco, Negroni Sbagliato, 42
Cinzano Rosso Vermouth, Martínez Spritz, 189
club soda
   Distant Call, 123
   Flash Gordon, 114
   Fruits of the Monastic Life, 117
   Paomo Ambrosia, 153
   Whistlepodu, 154
Cocchi Americano Rosa, Rosa Spritz, 62
Cocchi Vermouth Di Torino Extra Dry, Extra Sonic, 54
Cognac
   Fleur de Lis, 33
   Hidden Sweet, 213
   Ritz Spritz, 190

Cointreau, No One Mourns the Wicked, 177
Collins glass
   The Beehive, 157
   Beyond the Sea, 161
   Cherry Valance, 119
   Cucumber Collins, 170
   Diablo Otoño, 169
   Extra Sonic, 54
   Island Hopper, 118
   Milk Beach, 174
   Mining for Gold, 137
   Pacific Rhythms, 66
   Paloma, 106
   Pimm's Cup, 68
   Pink Sky, 72
   Purple Rain, 93
   Sideways, 86
   Tropical Bird Spritz, 206
   Very Hungry Manzanilla, 25
   Violet Skies, 152
Cometa recipe, 212
Cool as Moons recipe, 162
coupe
   Ananda Spritz, 17
   Berries & Bubbles, 113
   California Cooler, 194
   La Diosa, 166
   Floating Leaf, 101
   The Jerome, 205
   Lady in Red, 76
   Mystic Beauty, 210
   Pride, 201
   Ritz Spritz, 190
   Rose Blossom, 30
   Trench 75, 202
cranberries/cranberry juice
   Cool as Moons, 162
   The Marleybone Crush, 130
   Crème de Violette, Violet Skies, 152

Crystal Gazpacho recipe, 158
El Cuco recipe, 81
cucumber
   Apple of Your Eye, 18
   Botanical Garden Spritz, 21
   Crystal Gazpacho, 158
   Cucumber Collins, 170
   Cucumber & Rosé Highball, 98
   Cucumber Syrup, 99
   Pacific Rhythms, 66
   Pimm's Cup, 68
   Sacred Lotus, 26
Cucumber Collins recipe, 170
Cucumber & Rosé Highball recipe, 98
Cucumber Syrup recipe, 99
Curaçao, Ritz Spritz, 190

### D

Deci's Roommate recipe, 37
Demerara Syrup
   Ananda Spritz, 17
   Passion Fruit Syrup, 152
Demerara Syrup recipe, 16
Diablo Otoño recipe, 169
Diciotto recipe, 53
Disaronno Originale, Distant Call, 123
Distant Call recipe, 123
Dolin Blanc Vermouth, Sicilian Sbagliato, 45
El Dorado 3 Year Rum, El Cuco, 81
dry rosé, Summer Garden No. 1, 97
dry rosé wine, Sitting in Trees, 185
dry vermouth
   Botanical Garden Spritz, 21
   Crystal Gazpacho, 158

High C Spritz, 77
Lemon Thyme-Infused Vermouth, 75

**E**
edible flowers
Ananda Spritz, 17
Berries & Bubbles, 113
Botanical Garden Spritz, 21
Cometa, 212
La Diosa, 166
The Garden, 71
Orphic Flowers, 209
Pacific Rhythms, 66
Saffron Spritz, 182
Sgroppino Plagiato, 22
Sicilian Sbagliato, 45
edible gold leaf, Mining for Gold, 137
edible green leaf, Beverly Interpretation, 126
Effen Blood Orange Vodka, Brighter Days, 193
eggs
Brighter Days, 193
Farm & Vine, 29
Formosa Fizz, 69
Mystic Beauty, 210
Paomo Ambrosia, 153
Violet Skies, 152
elderflower liqueur
Elderflower Spritz, 14
I Wish I Was in New Orleans, 78
Elderflower Spritz recipe, 14
Elevate
Balearica, 178
The Beehive, 157
Beyond the Sea, 161
Bocanada, 181
Cauldron Cure, 165
Cool as Moons, 162
Crystal Gazpacho, 158
Cucumber Collins, 170
Diablo Otoño, 169
La Diosa, 166
Milk Beach, 174
No One Mourns the Wicked, 177
Paomo Ambrosia, 153
Saffron Spritz, 182
Seville Spritz, 173
Sitting in Trees, 185
Violet Skies, 152
Whistlepodu, 154
Excite
Americano, 38
Ananda Spritz, 17
Aperol Spritz, 10
Apple of Your Eye, 18
Botanical Garden Spritz, 21
Broken Bicyclette, 58
Campari Seltz, 49
Deci's Roommate, 37
Diciotto, 53
Elderflower Spritz, 14
Extra Sonic, 54
Farm & Vine, 29
Fleur de Lis, 33
Go Ahead, Romeo, 13
Italicus Cup, 57
Negroni Sbagliato, 42
Rosa Spritz, 62
Rose Blossom, 30
Sacred Lotus, 26
Select Spritz, 41
Sgroppino Plagiato, 22
Sicilian Sbagliato, 45
Sour Cherry Spritz, 61
Stazione, 46
Vermuttino, 50
Very Hungry Manzanilla, 25
Yokota, 34
Extra Sonic recipe, 54

**F**
Farm & Vine recipe, 29
Fennel-Infused Tequila recipe, 185
Fever-Tree Elderflower tonic water, Cucumber & Rosé Highball, 98
Fever-Tree Ginger Ale, Cherry Valance, 119
Fever-Tree Lemon tonic water, Pink Sky, 72
Fever-Tree Mediterranean tonic water
Basilico, 75
Saffron Spritz, 182
Fever-Tree Sparkling Lime & Yuzu, Pacific Rhythms, 66
Fever-Tree Sparkling Pink Grapefruit, St. Kilda, 90
Fig Cordial recipe, 168
Fig Leaf Syrup recipe, 168
fig liqueur, Diablo Otoño, 169
fino sherry
Bocanada, 181
Cometa, 212
Fiorente elderflower liqueur, Hugo, 85
Flash Gordon recipe, 114
Fleur de Lis recipe, 33
Floating Leaf recipe, 101
footed pilsner glass, Apple of Your Eye, 18
Formosa Fizz recipe, 69
47 Monkeys recipe, 197
French 75 recipe, 188
Fruits of the Monastic Life recipe, 117
Fruity Bag recipe, 89

**G**
Galliano Sambuca Black, No One Mourns the Wicked, 177
The Garden recipe, 71
Giffard Rhubarb Liqueur, Cool as Moons, 162
gin
Berries & Bubbles, 113
California Cooler, 194
French 75, 188
The Garden, 71
Gintarito, 138
Kaffir Lime Leaf-Infused Gin, 162
The Marleybone Crush, 130
Mi-Và, 129
Pink Strawberry Rosé, 102
Stazione, 46
Tea Time with Charley, 145
Violet Skies, 152
ginger
Ginger Syrup, 164
Honey & Ginger Syrup, 81
Masala Water, 155
ginger beer
Apple of Your Eye, 18
Island Hopper, 118
Summer Garden No. 1, 97
Ginger Solution recipe, 157
Ginger Syrup recipe, 164
Gintarito recipe, 138
glassware
brandy snifter
Go Ahead, Romeo, 13
Champagne coupe
Orphic Flowers, 209
Champagne flute
Basilico, 75
Bellini, 110
Beverly Interpretation, 126
Brighter Days, 193
Formosa Fizz, 69
French 75, 188
Hidden Sweet, 213

High C Spritz, 77
I Wish I Was in New Orleans, 78
Mimosa, 109
Port in a Storm, 198
Rossini, 120
Saffron Spritz, 182
Stranger Things, 82
Veruschka, 125
Collins glass
  The Beehive, 157
  Beyond the Sea, 161
  Cherry Valance, 119
  Cucumber Collins, 170
  Diablo Otoño, 169
  Extra Sonic, 54
  Island Hopper, 118
  Milk Beach, 174
  Mining for Gold, 137
  Pacific Rhythms, 66
  Paloma, 106
  Pimm's Cup, 68
  Pink Sky, 72
  Purple Rain, 93
  Sideways, 86
  Tropical Bird Spritz, 206
  Very Hungry Manzanilla, 25
  Violet Skies, 152
coupe
  Ananda Spritz, 17
  Berries & Bubbles, 113
  California Cooler, 194
  La Diosa, 166
  Floating Leaf, 101
  The Jerome, 205
  Lady in Red, 76
  Mystic Beauty, 210
  Pride, 201
  Ritz Spritz, 190
  Rose Blossom, 30
  Trench 75, 202
footed pilsner glass
  Apple of Your Eye, 18
goblet
  Balearica, 178
  Diciotto, 53
  Sgroppino Plagiato, 22
highball glass
  Broken Bicyclette, 58
  Cool as Moons, 162
  Cucumber & Rosé Highball, 98
  Flash Gordon, 114
  Fruits of the Monastic Life, 117
  Fruity Bag, 89
  Gintarito, 138
  Italicus Cup, 57
  Kissed By a Rose, 134
  The Marleybone Crush, 130
  Mind Games, 141
  Mi-Và, 129
  Nami Spritz, 94
  Pink Strawberry Rosé, 102
  Raspberry Beret, 146
  Rosa Spritz, 62
  Seville Spritz, 173
  Sicilian Sbagliato, 45
  Sitting in Trees, 185
  St. Kilda, 90
  Summer Garden No. 1, 97
  Sunlit Horizon, 149
  Vermuttino, 50
lightbulb glass
  Stranger Things, 82
rocks glass
  Americano, 38
  Aroma, 122
  Bocanada, 181
  Cometa, 212
  El Cuco, 81
  Deci's Roommate, 37
  Farm & Vine, 29
  Fleur de Lis, 33
  Paomo Ambrosia, 153
  Piscomelo, 142
  Whistlepodu, 154
snifter
  Cauldron Cure, 165
tulip glass
  Campari Seltz, 49
tumbler
  The Garden, 71
  Stazione, 46
white wineglass
  Distant Call, 123
  Select Spritz, 41
  Yokota, 34
wineglass
  47 Monkeys, 197
  Aperol Spritz, 10
  Botanical Garden Spritz, 21
  Crystal Gazpacho, 158
  Elderflower Spritz, 14
  Hugo, 85
  Martínez Spritz, 189
  Negroni Sbagliato, 42
  No One Mourns the Wicked, 177
  Running Up That Hill, 133
  Sacred Lotus, 26
  Sour Cherry Spritz, 61
  Tea Time with Charley, 145
Go Ahead, Romeo recipe, 13
goblet
  Balearica, 178
  Diciotto, 53
  Sgroppino Plagiato, 22
  Gordon's London Dry Gin, Flash Gordon, 114
grapefruit/grapefruit juice
  Aroma, 122
  Balearica, 178
Beverly Interpretation, 126
El Cuco, 81
Diciotto, 53
Elderflower Spritz, 14
House Tajín, 167
Italicus Cup, 57
Mi-Và, 129
Paloma, 106
Pink Sky, 72
Piscomelo, 142
Port in a Storm, 198
Running Up That Hill, 133
Sunlit Horizon, 149
Triple Citrus-Infused Gin, 165
grapefruit soda
  Gintarito, 138
  Italicus Cup, 57
  Piscomelo, 142
Grappa Nonino Monovitigno Merlot, Sideways, 86
Green Chartreuse, Fruits of the Monastic Life, 117
Green Raicilla recipe, 181
grenadine
  Balearica, 178
  Strawberry Vinegar, 76
Griottine, Cherry Valance, 119

## H

Hamilton Guyana 86 Rum, El Cuco, 81
Havana Club 7 Year Rum, I Wish I Was in New Orleans, 78
Hendrick's Gin, Apple of Your Eye, 18
Hendrick's Orbium Gin, Olive Leaf-Infused Gin, 77
Hibiscus Syrup recipe, 118
Hidden Sweet recipe, 213

highball glass
   Broken Bicyclette, 58
   Cool as Moons, 162
   Cucumber & Rosé Highball, 98
   Flash Gordon, 114
   Fruits of the Monastic Life, 117
   Fruity Bag, 89
   Gintarito, 138
   Italicus Cup, 57
   Kissed By a Rose, 134
   The Marleybone Crush, 130
   Mind Games, 141
   Mi-Và, 129
   Nami Spritz, 94
   Pink Strawberry Rosé, 102
   Raspberry Beret, 146
   Rosa Spritz, 62
   Seville Spritz, 173
   Sicilian Sbagliato, 45
   Sitting in Trees, 185
   St. Kilda, 90
   Summer Garden No. 1, 97
   Sunlit Horizon, 149
   Vermuttino, 50
High C Spritz recipe, 77
honey
   Fig Cordial, 168
   Honey & Ginger Syrup, 81
   Honey Water, 33
   Saffron Honey, 183
   Sarsaparilla-Infused Honey Syrup, 156
   Seaweed-Infused Honey, 161
   Whistlepodu, 154
Honey & Ginger Syrup recipe, 81
Honey Water
   Fleur de Lis, 33
   Trench 75, 202

Honey Water recipe, 33
House Tajín recipe, 167
Hugo recipe, 85

### I
Indian Sarsaparilla, Sarsaparilla-Infused Honey Syrup, 156
Island Hopper recipe, 118
Italicus Cup recipe, 57
Italicus Rosolio Di Bergamotto
   Beverly Interpretation, 126
   Italicus Cup, 57
   Milk Beach, 174
   Rose Blossom, 30
   I Wish I Was in New Orleans recipe, 78

### J
Jasmine-Infused Vodka recipe, 200
The Jerome recipe, 205

### K
Kaffir Lime Leaf-Infused Gin recipe, 162
kale
   Bocanada, 181
   Green Raicilla, 181
Kamm & Sons British Aperitif, Botanical Garden Spritz, 21
Kissed By a Rose recipe, 134
Knob Creek Bourbon, Ananda Spritz, 17

### L
Lady in Red recipe, 76
lemons/lemon juice
   Ananda Spritz, 17
   Apple of Your Eye, 18
   The Beehive, 157
   Bellini, 110
   Berries & Bubbles, 113
   Beyond the Sea, 161

   Brighter Days, 193
   Cauldron Cure, 165
   Cometa, 212
   Cool as Moons, 162
   Cucumber Collins, 170
   Cucumber & Rosé Highball, 98
   Distant Call, 123
   Flash Gordon, 114
   Fleur de Lis, 33
   Floating Leaf, 101
   Formosa Fizz, 69
   French 75, 188
   The Garden, 71
   Gintarito, 138
   Island Hopper, 118
   I Wish I Was in New Orleans, 78
   The Jerome, 205
   Kissed By a Rose, 134
   Milk Beach, 174
   Mind Games, 141
   Mining for Gold, 137
   Mystic Beauty, 210
   Nami Spritz, 94
   Pacific Rhythms, 66
   Paomo Ambrosia, 153
   Pimm's Cup, 68
   Pink Strawberry Rosé, 102
   Piscomelo, 142
   Purple Rain, 93
   Ritz Spritz, 190
   Rossini, 120
   Sacred Lotus, 26
   Saffron Spritz, 182
   Sitting in Trees, 185
   Strawberry Vinegar, 76
   Sweet & Sour, 129
   Trench 75, 202
   Triple Citrus-Infused Gin, 165
   Tropical Fruit Sorbet, 23
   Vermuttino, 50

Violet Skies, 152
Yokota, 34
Lemon Thyme-Infused Vermouth recipe, 75
lightbulb glass, Stranger Things, 82
Lillet Blanc
   Nami Spritz, 94
   Pineapple Marmalade, 166
Lime & Sage Cordial recipe, 200
limes/lime juice
   47 Monkeys, 197
   Apple of Your Eye, 18
   Balearica, 178
   Beyond the Sea, 161
   Bocanada, 181
   California Cooler, 194
   Cherry Valance, 119
   Cool as Moons, 162
   El Cuco, 81
   Deci's Roommate, 37
   La Diosa, 166
   Farm & Vine, 29
   Fruits of the Monastic Life, 117
   Gintarito, 138
   Island Hopper, 118
   I Wish I Was in New Orleans, 78
   Lime & Sage Cordial, 200
   The Marleybone Crush, 130
   Negroni Sbagliato, 42
   Pacific Rhythms, 66
   Paloma, 106
   Pink Sky, 72
   Pink Strawberry Rosé, 102
   Raspberry Beret, 146
   Raspberry Cordial, 92
   Running Up That Hill, 133
   Sideways, 86
   Stazione, 46

St. Kilda, 90
Summer Garden No. 1, 97
Sweet & Sour, 129
Tea Time with Charley recipe, 145
Tropical Bird Spritz, 206
Very Hungry Manzanilla, 25
Whistlepodu, 154

limoncello
 Aroma, 122
 Mining for Gold, 137
 Sicilian Sbagliato, 45

London dry gin
 Botanical Garden Spritz, 21
 Cucumber & Rosé Highball, 98
 Lady in Red, 76
 Mind Games, 141
 Mystic Beauty, 210
 Triple Citrus-Infused Gin, 165

Lustau Moscatel sherry, Yokota, 34
Luxardo Bitter Bianco, Sicilian Sbagliato, 45
Luxardo Maraschino Liqueur
 Pacific Rhythms, 66
 Ritz Spritz, 190

## M

mango/mango puree
 Masala Water, 155
 Tropical Fruit Sorbet, 23

manzanilla sherry
 Farm & Vine, 29
 Very Hungry Manzanilla, 25

maraschino cherry
 Cool as Moons, 162
 French 75, 188
 Mind Games, 141

Marendry Amarena Wild Cherry Aperitivo, Sour Cherry Spritz, 61
The Marleybone Crush recipe, 130
Martínez Spritz recipe, 189
Martini & Rossi Riserva Prosecco, Tropical Bird Spritz, 206
Martini & Rossi Riserva Speciale Bitter Vermouth, Tropical Bird Spritz, 206
Martini & Rossi Rosso Sweet Vermouth, Vermuttino, 50
Masala Water recipe, 155
Melon Juice recipe, 184
mezcal, Cometa, 212
Midori, Pacific Rhythms, 66
Milk Beach recipe, 174
Mimosa recipe, 109
Mind Games recipe, 141
Mining for Gold recipe, 137

mint
 Apple of Your Eye, 18
 Aroma, 122
 Cool as Moons, 162
 El Cuco, 81
 Deci's Roommate, 37
 Extra Sonic, 54
 Hugo, 85
 Masala Water, 155
 Pacific Rhythms, 66
 Pimm's Cup, 68
 Raspberry Beret, 146
 Sacred Lotus, 26
 Sage & Mint Agave, 24
 Sideways, 86
 Very Hungry Manzanilla, 25

Mi-Và recipe, 129
Monkey 47 Schwarzwald Dry Gin, 47 Monkeys, 197

Monkey 47 Schwarzwald Sloe Gin, 47 Monkeys, 197
Mystic Beauty recipe, 210

## N

Nami Spritz recipe, 94
Negroni Sbagliato recipe, 42
Nikka Coffey Gin, Trench 75, 202
No One Mourns the Wicked recipe, 177

nori
 Beyond the Sea, 161
 Seaweed-Infused Honey, 161

## O

Oakland Spirits Co. Automatic Sea Gin, Beyond the Sea, 161
Olive Leaf-Infused Gin recipe, 77

orange bitters
 The Beehive, 157
 Seville Spritz, 173

oranges/orange juice
 Americano, 38
 Aperol Spritz, 10
 Fleur de Lis, 33
 Gintarito, 138
 Go Ahead, Romeo, 13
 Italicus Cup, 57
 Mimosa, 109
 Pimm's Cup, 68
 Pineapple Marmalade, 166
 Purple Rain, 93
 Ritz Spritz, 190
 Sacred Lotus, 26
 Seville Spritz, 173
 Tea Time with Charley, 145
 Triple Citrus-Infused Gin, 165

orange wine, Seville Spritz, 173
orgeat, Violet Skies, 152
Orphic Flowers recipe, 209

## P

Pacific Rhythms recipe, 66
Paloma recipe, 106
Paomo Ambrosia recipe, 153

passion fruit/passion fruit juice
 Kissed By a Rose, 134
 Martínez Spritz, 189
 Passion Fruit Rosé, 134
 Passion Fruit Syrup, 152
 Stranger Things, 82
 Tropical Fruit Sorbet, 23

Passion Fruit Rosé recipe, 134
Passion Fruit Syrup recipe, 152

peach nectar
 Bellini, 110
 Broken Bicyclette, 58

pear brandy, Cool as Moons, 162

peppers
 Masala Water, 155
 Pineapple Marmalade, 166
 Thai Pepper Shrub, 72

Peychaud's bitters
 47 Monkeys, 197
 Apple of Your Eye, 18
 Fleur de Lis, 33
 I Wish I Was in New Orleans, 78
 The Jerome, 205
 Rose Blossom, 30

Pickled Huckleberries recipe, 171
Pickled Purple Cucumbers recipe, 171

Pierre Ferrand Cognac, The Jerome, 205
Pierre Ferrand Dry Curaçao, Seville Spritz, 173
Pimm's Cup recipe, 68
Pimm's No. 1
  Apple of Your Eye, 18
  Pimm's Cup, 68
Pineapple Marmalade recipe, 166
pineapple/pineapple juice
  Ananda Spritz, 17
  Island Hopper, 118
  Pineapple Marmalade, 166
  Pineapple Shrub, 206
Pink Strawberry Rosé recipe, 102
Piscomelo recipe, 142
Plantation 3 Stars Rum, Very Hungry Manzanilla, 25
Port in a Storm recipe, 198
Pride recipe, 201
prosecco
  Aperol Spritz, 10
  Brighter Days, 193
  Elderflower Spritz, 14
  Go Ahead, Romeo, 13
  Hugo, 85
  Mystic Beauty, 210
  Negroni Sbagliato, 42
  Rosa Spritz, 62
  Rossini, 120
  Sacred Lotus, 26
  Select Spritz, 41
  Seville Spritz, 173
  Sgroppino Plagiato, 22
  Sicilian Sbagliato, 45
  Sour Cherry Spritz, 61
  Stranger Things, 82
  Veruschka, 125
Purple Rain recipe, 93

## Q
Q Elderflower tonic, Farm & Vine, 29
Q tonic water, The Garden, 71

## R
raspberries
  Berries & Bubbles, 113
  Formosa Fizz, 69
  Raspberry Beret, 146
  Raspberry Cordial, 92
  Raspberry Shrub, 210
  Raspberry Syrup, 69
  Stranger Things, 82
Raspberry Beret recipe, 146
Raspberry Cordial recipe, 92
Raspberry Shrub recipe, 210
Raspberry Syrup recipe, 69
Refresh
  Basilico, 75
  El Cuco, 81
  Cucumber & Rosé Highball, 98
  Floating Leaf, 101
  Formosa Fizz, 69
  Fruity Bag, 89
  The Garden, 71
  High C Spritz, 77
  Hugo, 85
  I Wish I Was in New Orleans, 78
  Lady in Red, 76
  Nami Spritz, 94
  Pacific Rhythms, 66
  Pimm's Cup, 68
  Pink Sky, 72
  Pink Strawberry Rosé, 102
  Purple Rain, 93
  Sideways, 86
  St. Kilda, 90
  Stranger Things, 82
  Summer Garden No. 1, 97
Relax
  Aroma, 122
  Bellini, 110
  Berries & Bubbles, 113
  Beverly Interpretation, 126
  Cherry Valance, 119
  Distant Call, 123
  Flash Gordon, 114
  Fruits of the Monastic Life, 117
  Gintarito, 138
  Island Hopper, 118
  Kissed By a Rose, 134
  The Marleybone Crush, 130
  Mimosa, 109
  Mind Games, 141
  Mining for Gold, 137
  Mi-Và, 129
  Paloma, 106
  Piscomelo, 142
  Raspberry Beret, 146
  Rossini, 120
  Running Up That Hill, 133
  Sunlit Horizon, 149
  Tea Time with Charley, 145
  Veruschka, 125
Rhum Agricole, Island Hopper, 118
Rich Simple Syrup
  Deci's Roommate, 37
  Formosa Fizz, 69
  The Jerome, 205
  Kissed By a Rose, 134
  Raspberry Beret, 146
  Sweet & Sour, 129
  Violet Skies, 152
Rich Simple Syrup recipe, 37
Ritz Spritz recipe, 190
rocks glass
  Americano, 38
  Aroma, 122
  Bocanada, 181
  Cometa, 212
  El Cuco, 81
  Deci's Roommate, 37
  Farm & Vine, 29
  Fleur de Lis, 33
  Paomo Ambrosia, 153
  Piscomelo, 142
  Whistlepodu, 154
Rosa Spritz recipe, 62
rosé
  Apple-Infused Rosé, 182
  Berries & Bubbles, 113
  Cucumber & Rosé Highball, 98
  Deci's Roommate, 37
  Floating Leaf, 101
  Pink Strawberry Rosé, 102
  Raspberry Beret, 146
  Rosé & Strawberry Syrup, 89
  Summer Garden No. 1, 97
  Sunlit Horizon, 149
Rose Blossom recipe, 30
rosé Champagne, Hidden Sweet, 213
rosemary
  Crystal Gazpacho, 158
  Elderflower Spritz, 14
  Paloma, 106
  Rosemary Syrup, 96
  Running Up That Hill, 133
  Summer Garden No. 1, 97
Rosemary Syrup recipe, 96
Rosé & Strawberry Syrup recipe, 89
Rose Syrup recipe, 71
Rossini recipe, 120

Running Up That Hill recipe, 133

### S

Sacred Lotus recipe, 26
Saffron Honey recipe, 183
Saffron Spritz recipe, 182
sage
 Cherry Valance, 119
 Lime & Sage Cordial, 200
 Sage & Mint Agave, 24
Sage & Mint Agave recipe, 24
sake
 Nami Spritz, 94
 Paomo Ambrosia, 153
 Pickled Huckleberries, 171
 Trench 75, 202
San Pellegrino, Sicilian Sbagliato, 45
San Pellegrino Limonata, Mining for Gold, 137
Sarsaparilla-Infused Honey Syrup recipe, 156
Sauvignon Blanc & Thyme Cordial recipe, 195
Seaweed-Infused Honey recipe, 161
Select Aperitivo
 Broken Bicyclette, 58
 Select Spritz, 41
 Sgroppino Plagiato, 22
Select Spritz recipe, 41
seltzer
 Aperol Spritz, 10
 Hugo, 85
seltzer water
 Campari Seltz, 49
 El Cuco, 81
 Very Hungry Manzanilla, 25
Seville Spritz recipe, 173
shiso leaf
 Farm & Vine, 29
 Paomo Ambrosia, 153

Sicilian Sbagliato recipe, 45
Sideways recipe, 86
silver tequila
 Formosa Fizz, 69
 Running Up That Hill, 133
 St. Kilda, 90
Simple Syrup
 Banana Syrup, 153
 Berries & Bubbles, 113
 Brighter Days, 193
 Cucumber Collins, 170
 Fig Leaf Syrup, 168
 Flash Gordon, 114
 Hibiscus Syrup, 118
 Martínez Spritz, 189
 Milk Beach, 174
 Mind Games, 141
 Mining for Gold, 137
 Pacific Rhythms, 66
 Purple Rain, 93
 Running Up That Hill, 133
 Sideways, 86
 Stranger Things, 82
 Strawberry Vinegar, 76
 Yokota, 34
Simple Syrup recipe, 34
Sitting in Trees recipe, 185
Smoked Rasam recipe, 154
snifter, Cauldron Cure, 165
soda water
 Americano, 38
 The Beehive, 157
 Beyond the Sea, 161
 Botanical Garden Spritz, 21
 Broken Bicyclette, 58
 Cometa, 212
 Crystal Gazpacho, 158
 Cucumber Collins, 170
 La Diosa, 166
 Extra Sonic, 54

Formosa Fizz, 69
Kissed By a Rose, 134
Mind Games, 141
No One Mourns the Wicked, 177
Purple Rain, 93
Raspberry Beret, 146
Select Spritz, 41
Sideways, 86
Sitting in Trees, 185
Sour Cherry Spritz, 61
Sunlit Horizon, 149
Tropical Bird Spritz, 206
Vermuttino, 50
Sour Cherry Spritz recipe, 61
sparkling rosé
 Berries & Bubbles, 113
 Deci's Roommate, 37
 Floating Leaf, 101
 Pink Strawberry Rosé, 102
 Sunlit Horizon, 149
sparkling water
 Balearica, 178
 Nami Spritz, 94
 Rosa Spritz, 62
 Violet Skies, 152
sparkling wine
 Ananda Spritz, 17
 Cool as Moons, 162
 Fleur de Lis, 33
 Lady in Red, 76
 Martínez Spritz, 189
 Rose Blossom, 30
 Tea Time with Charley, 145
Square One Cucumber Vodka, Cucumber Collins, 170
Stazione recipe, 46
St-Germain
 Botanical Garden Spritz, 21

Bread St-Germain, 159
Pink Sky, 72
Sacred Lotus, 26
Tea Time with Charley, 145
Tropical Bird Spritz, 206
St. Kilda recipe, 90
Stranger Things recipe, 82
strawberries
 47 Monkeys, 197
 Fruity Bag, 89
 Pimm's Cup, 68
 Rosa Spritz, 62
 Rosé & Strawberry Syrup, 89
 Rossini, 120
 Strawberry-Infused Vodka, 100
 Strawberry Syrup, 102
 Strawberry Vinegar, 76
Strawberry-Infused Vodka recipe, 100
Strawberry Syrup recipe, 102
Strawberry Tea-Infused Vodka recipe, 82
Strawberry Vinegar recipe, 76
Strega
 Diciotto, 53
 Stazione, 46
Sugar Snap Pea Syrup recipe, 28
Summer Garden No. 1 recipe, 97
Sunlit Horizon recipe, 149
Suze
 High C Spritz, 77
 The Jerome, 205
sweet rosé, Cucumber & Rosé Highball, 98
Sweet & Sour recipe, 129
sweet vermouth, Pineapple Marmalade, 166

**T**

Tamarind-Infused Vodka recipe, 26
Tanqueray No. Ten
    Balearica, 178
    Basilico, 75
    Rose Blossom, 30
Tanqueray Sevilla Orange, Seville Spritz, 173
Tea Time with Charley recipe, 145
10 Percent Saline Solution recipe, 156
tequila
    Diablo Otoño, 169
    La Diosa, 166
    Fennel-Infused Tequila, 185
    Formosa Fizz, 69
    Paloma, 106
    Pink Sky, 72
    Port in a Storm, 198
    Running Up That Hill, 133
    St. Kilda, 90
Thai Pepper Shrub recipe, 72
Three Cents Gentlemen's Soda, High C Spritz, 77
thyme
    Broken Bicyclette, 58
    Lemon Thyme-Infused Vermouth, 75
    Sauvignon Blanc & Thyme Cordial, 195
tomatoes
    Crystal Gazpacho, 158
    Smoked Rasam, 154
    Tomato Gin, 158
    Tomato Shrub, 159
Tomato Gin recipe, 158
Tomato Shrub recipe, 159
tonic water
    Aroma, 122

Basilico, 75
Bocanada, 181
Crystal Gazpacho, 158
Cucumber & Rosé Highball, 98
Diablo Otoño, 169
Extra Sonic, 54
The Garden, 71
Pink Sky, 72
Saffron Spritz, 182
Stazione, 46
Topo Chico, Running Up That Hill, 133
Trench 75 recipe, 202
Triple Citrus-Infused Gin recipe, 165
triple sec, La Diosa, 166
Tropical Bird Spritz recipe, 206
Tropical Fruit Sorbet recipe, 23
tulip glass, Campari Seltz, 49
tumbler
    The Garden, 71
    Stazione, 46

**U**

Umeboshi Powder, Farm & Vine, 29
Umeboshi Powder recipe, 28

**V**

Vanilla Syrup
    Gintarito, 138
    Seville Spritz, 173
    Sitting in Trees, 185
Vanilla Syrup recipe, 138
verjus
    Farm & Vine, 29
    Fleur de Lis, 33
    The Jerome, 205
vermouth
    Americano, 38

Botanical Garden Spritz, 21
Crystal Gazpacho, 158
High C Spritz, 77
Lemon Thyme-Infused Vermouth, 75
Martínez Spritz, 189
Negroni Sbagliato, 42
Pineapple Marmalade, 166
Sicilian Sbagliato, 45
Tropical Bird Spritz, 206
Vermuttino, 50
Vermuttino recipe, 50
Veruschka recipe, 125
Violet Skies recipe, 152
vodka
    Berries & Bubbles, 113
    Cherry Valance, 119
    Fruity Bag, 89
    Jasmine-Infused Vodka, 200
    Mining for Gold, 137
    Purple Rain, 93
    Raspberry Beret, 146
    Sour Cherry Spritz, 61
    Strawberry-Infused Vodka, 100
    Strawberry Tea-Infused Vodka, 82
    Tamarind-Infused Vodka, 26
    Veruschka, 125
    Whistlepodu, 154

**W**

watermelon
    St. Kilda, 90
    Summer Garden No. 1, 97
    Watermelon Shrub, 90
Watermelon Shrub recipe, 90
Whistlepodu recipe, 154
white wine
    Broken Bicyclette, 58

Martínez Spritz, 189
white wineglass
    Distant Call, 123
    Select Spritz, 41
    Yokota, 34
wineglass
    47 Monkeys, 197
    Aperol Spritz, 10
    Botanical Garden Spritz, 21
    Crystal Gazpacho, 158
    Elderflower Spritz, 14
    Hugo, 85
    Martínez Spritz, 189
    Negroni Sbagliato, 42
    No One Mourns the Wicked, 177
    Running Up That Hill, 133
    Sacred Lotus, 26
    Sour Cherry Spritz, 61
    Tea Time with Charley, 145

**Y**

Yokota recipe, 34
yuzu juice
    Cucumber Collins, 170
    Paomo Ambrosia, 153

## ABOUT CIDER MILL PRESS BOOK PUBLISHERS

Good ideas ripen with time. From seed to harvest, Cider Mill Press brings fine reading, information, and entertainment together between the covers of its creatively crafted books. Our Cider Mill bears fruit twice a year, publishing a new crop of titles each spring and fall.

"Where Good Books Are Ready for Press"
501 Nelson Place
Nashville, Tennessee 37214

cidermillpress.com